T0199154

# TENSION
# THEOLOGY

The Tension Is in the Scriptures . . .
When We Remove It,
That Makes for More Tension Between Us

## B.D.Tate

WESTBOW
P R E S S®
A DIVISION OF THOMAS NELSON
& ZONDERVAN

Scripture taken from the New King James Version. Copyright © 1979, 1980,
1982 by Thomas Nelson, Inc. Used by permission. All rights reserved.

Scripture quotations marked (AV) are taken from
the Authorized Version of the Bible.

WestBow Press books may be ordered through booksellers or by contacting:

WestBow Press
A Division of Thomas Nelson & Zondervan
1663 Liberty Drive
Bloomington, IN 47403
www.westbowpress.com
1 (866) 928-1240

ISBN: 978-1-5127-5838-2 (sc)
ISBN: 978-1-5127-5839-9 (hc)
ISBN: 978-1-5127-5837-5 (e)

Library of Congress Control Number: 2016916365

Print information available on the last page.

WestBow Press rev. date: 12/9/2016

# DEDICATION

This book, Tension Theology, is dedicated to the encouragement, support, and push from my wife. It is also in dedication to the many brothers and sisters whose work I've read, sermons I've heard, and discussions we've shared over the years.

# Epigraph

"I like books that bring people together!" Greg F. Tate

# CONTENTS

# FOREWORD

For many years, I lived a paralyzed, fearful Christian life. I loved Jesus, and trusted God, but watched my mother struggle for decades with Multiple Sclerosis. She was a wonderful Christian woman. I didn't understand why she wasn't healed. I was told that sometimes God allows bad things to happen in people's lives so they learn to walk more closely with Him.

That scared me. I began to worry that God might send a terrible disease on me, or one of my loved ones, to somehow "prove" our devotion. I wanted to serve God, I wanted to know Him in a deeper way—but what if that involved suffering like my mother did? My prayers became long lists of diseases I begged God not to send on my family or me. I lived in a haze of doubt and worry.

Then God, in His mercy, led me to Lord of Lords Bible Community Church, where I came under the teaching and leadership of Pastor Tate. He helped me to see the same scriptures I had read all my life from a different perspective.

I learned about the "tension" of scripture, and how falling too far to one side of the issue of suffering had caused all the confusion in my life. I learned that the seeming "contradictions" in the Word actually create a bigger picture, a balance. Staying balanced in the center of this tension keeps us in a place of peace, where we are free to rest in God's protection and bask in His love.

This new way of approaching scripture absolutely changed my life. With new eyes, I could understand how the Old Testament law fit with New Testament grace, as well as the balance between God's plan for our lives, and our own free will. I had a better grasp on why and how bad things happen, and how God has given me—and you—the authority to intervene.

This approach has been so life-changing for our church, that we encouraged Pastor Tate to get the word out to other struggling Christians, and write this book.

I pray that seeing scripture in this new light will change your life as well, dear reader, freeing your heart to know God better, and to grow in His grace.

Adele R. Shaw
June 20, 2016

# PREFACE

Tension Theology came into being because the scriptures contain what many might call contradictions. The Bible is filled with teachings that state themes in opposing ways. On the one hand, the Bible is clear to reveal a concept; on the other hand, it reveals something almost opposite regarding the same issue. The more we understand scripture, the more we run into tensions.

Most of us typically ignore, overlook, or discount one side over the other side. We often employ the either/or scenario versus accepting both. The question becomes: how can both of these opposing points concerning an issue be true? In our human understanding, we generally cannot figure out the answers. It is difficult, if not impossible, for our carnal minds to discern (I Cor. 2:14). Revelation knowledge is the work of the Holy Spirit, but we must be in the best place to receive.

When we remove the tension regarding any subject or issue found in scripture, we short circuit God's work in our lives. We are not in the best place to take in revelation. When we deny one scripture to affirm another scripture, it doesn't work well. Sometimes we must stand in both, acknowledge both, and wait for the Spirit's answers.

Many of our denominational divides begin with affirming one side of an issue, such as: God's Sovereignty versus human will; are we made righteous or progressing towards righteousness? Christianity is unique because of these tensions: Is Jesus God, or is He only human? The Trinity itself creates great confusion and much tension: are there three Gods or three distinct personages in one God?

Safety, security, and amazing answers come when we remain in the tensions. The truth is that any revelation of God breeds tension within our human understanding. How can finite beings comprehend the infinite? We do and we don't—it's both!

Tension Theology helps to explain why the tensions exist in the first place. It also warns us to embrace it as God's way to keep us on the straight and narrow road of truth in Christ. We might have the misconception that God's word, the gospel, and the revelation of grace, will all be simple, easy to grasp and have no conflict, but that is not the case. We are fallen, we live in a rebellious world, our sin nature opposes the things of the Spirit (Gal. 5:17); therefore, understand that the things of God will create in us tension. It is actually a good sign, a good position, and indicates that we are on the right track.

Ultimately, recognizing the tensions found in scripture will keep us from becoming puffed up, prideful and full of ourselves, because it takes humility to receive. It takes humility to remain in the tensions. Tension Theology: It's both, not either/or.

# ACKNOWLEDGMENT

I want to acknowledge a good friend, a wonderful sister in the Lord, and her tireless work of editing, encouraging, and sharing, which helped produce and make this book what it has become—Adele, thank you.

# INTRODUCTION

Christianity is rife with disagreements. Hardly one person completely agrees with another. Theologians group together under umbrellas of collective agreement. Churches associate in camps. Why are there such various interpretations *even* from the same passages of scripture?

We all believe that the other guy has it wrong. We point the finger to poor scholarship, taking things out of context, ignoring the whole counsel of God's word, or just being too biased, dogmatic, or entrenched in pride. All of this creates tension among us, when the culprit has often been our efforts to remove the tension found in scripture.

This book is called *Tension Theology* because in my nearly four decades of ministry (serving in churches and as a pastor), I have seen this phenomenon repeated over and over: removing the tension found in scripture. Many skeptics, critics, and agnostics, along with some believers, call these things contradictions. These *apparent* contradictions present opposing themes throughout the Bible's teaching. In essence, the tension created by the truth found in the revelations causes us discomfort. It is when we remove the discomfort within ourselves in addressing scripture that we end up to the left or to the right of the matter.

One way of looking at this is that God has placed tension in the revelations for our safety, to keep us on the straight and narrow road of who He is. We often remove it by emphasizing portions we like over portions we don't. We discount or ignore portions that don't agree with our narrative. When we remove the tension, we *fail to remain in the place where spiritual answers come.*

The fundamental question that always arises is this: *"How can these apparently contradictive passages both be true?"* It is in waiting, remaining faithful to both, that spiritual life and insight are revealed. It is when we don't do these things that we end up interpreting scripture from a natural, or *carnal,* mind set. It really leaves us underdeveloped in our theologies—even immature.

If we remain in the tension God has provided, we'll all find ourselves closer to the truth, and to each other. In this book, I explain the problem, and I present the theology of tension. Then I apply it to many well known controversies from the teachings of the body of Christ. Our battles often rage because we removed this tension from the scriptures, only to create it with each other. The message of this book will provide understanding, encouragement, and help for many, by recalculating their own theology with this principle in mind. It will help bring people together by staying in the tension, instead of choosing sides. When we separate the tension that scripture poses, we end up separating from each other.

This tension not only applies to the scriptures, it applies to many areas of life. For example, in the political arena, so many of us are familiar with the right and the left. The right is considered conservative, fundamental, remaining faithful to the original intent of the constitution, the bill of rights, and the writings of the founding fathers. The left is considered to be liberal, progressive, looking to adapt to changes, growing from the original intent of the constitution, the bill of rights, and the writings of the founding fathers, because the world has changed. The tension has often portrayed them as enemies, the opposition, partisan, and polar extremes. Each side has truth, and each side is denying it.

It's a peculiar reality, but the extremes are interpreted as being strong, full of conviction, convinced, unwavering, and ideological. The middle ground is seen as compromise, lacking vision, pragmatic, and someone with less conviction. These people are seen as less committed to deep thinking, almost superficial; however, it is really the opposite!

When we draw the conclusion that our convictions supersede the other side, we are standing in truth, but also negating it. When we are unwilling to see the position being presented by those we disagree with, we are lacking strength, lacking development, and lacking courage.

The tension in politics is often winner takes all. This causes us to jerk to the right or to the left as a country, depending on who is in power. Those who are acknowledging both sides, both opposing issues, are the moderates; they are trying to bring issues together. When they do, they bring others together.

The tension in politics includes many more things: agendas, propaganda, sin nature, and worldly versus godly priorities; yet, even so, the principle I'm writing about can be clearly seen, and applied, in the political realm.

Today, we often hear this from very important leaders, "Washington is broken!" What we really have is the tension being intensified because political leadership separates us to one side or the other. We are not being led to remain in the tension to find solutions that will remain, solutions that will work because they acknowledge conflicting truths. In the purest sense, we need both sides coming together to keep our nation on the straight and narrow.

## The Problem

We don't agree. I am amazed at the different places Christians of good heart find themselves. Not only do denominations not agree, but hardly one person agrees with another in depth. It is like going to a smorgasbord where everyone is choosing from the same variety, but no one comes up with the exact same assortment.

Why do we have such across the board divergence in Christianity? We're talking a large range, a broad road, and a massive highway of beliefs, all claiming to be proper interpretations of Biblical truth. How is it possible? Some have resigned it to human capacities to justify, rationalize, and reason fallibly, and of course we are talking about the other guy. Many claim it is poor scholarship, unfaithfulness to context, and a willful spirit (often caused by personal hurt, pain, and rejection).

Then the broad road includes a whole scope of interpretations based on reason, experience, and tradition, sometimes *over* the scriptural text. In some cases, liberal scholars claim that the Bible itself is fallible. However, to deny scripture's testimony in any one place is like opening Pandora's Box. When this occurs, what then are the constraints? Where do we draw a line of authority for sustaining our beliefs?

When does it become "anything goes" (what is best in our own eyes)? It is when scripture is no longer authoritative, or when it is piecemeal applied. We are all guilty of emphasizing some scriptures over and against others. Quite frankly, the Bible is too big, too much, and too deep for us to interpret it on our own.

> "As iron sharpens iron, *so a man sharpens the countenance* of his friend." (Proverbs 27:17, emphasis added)

Certainly, we must all realize that our finite understanding is dependent upon the contribution of others. It's like the four blind men who described what it was like to touch an elephant: one touched the tail, one touched the trunk, another blind man touched the ear, and the last one touched a leg, each adamantly insisting they were correct (and they were!); yet, each totally different in describing what they experienced. Obviously, the need to collaborate, and bring their descriptions together, would give them a far better grasp of what an elephant is.

That is simple enough, but the struggle I'm describing now isn't about touching different parts of scripture. It is about addressing the same places. We are describing the same issues, teachings, scriptures, and coming away adamantly insisting we are correct, and finding many disagreements. The result of which is often an impasse—the tension between us.

The impasse has many aspects. There is the human pride of being right. There is the assumption that the way we see things is the way they are (Pr. 14:12). There is the semantics problem of meaning, and sometimes redefining it. There are preconceived ideas. Not to be forgotten is our own background, upbringing, imprinting, and embracing of truth, because of what we were taught, and by whom.

In other words, virtues such as loyalty, faithfulness, trust, emotional attachment to a person, a church, and a teaching, are sometimes the hindrance to understanding and openness to truth. "My father is a great man, he couldn't be wrong!" Replace "father" with any person, a church pastor, a church, or a denomination, and this may unveil emotional attachments that can sometimes blind us, preventing growth in our understanding.

The tension causes us to withdraw from, distrust, disassociate, discontinue discussion, and emotionally distance ourselves from others. We all need affirmation, confirmation, a sense of belonging, and a place of agreement; it's not hard to understand why our differences lead to denominations, independent churches, and isolation for individuals. As my father once jested, "I'm still looking for a Bible I can agree with!"

I think we struggle so much with our beliefs because we are ignorant, easily confused, and easily misled—all of us. I think this is the "sheep" syndrome that Jesus referred to when He proclaimed He was the "good" shepherd. Sheep may be cute, but they are not the sharpest animal God created. Shepherds must be diligent to watch over them, for they easily stray away.

This is compounded by the fact that we compare ourselves among ourselves. There are smart sheep, intelligent, well educated, and very arrogant sheep; there are some who think they are no longer sheep, they are now shepherds. When did they stop being a sheep? When did their natural heart stop being deceitful, and desperately wicked? I remember hearing one Seminary professor make the claim, "We are all seeking truth!" Maybe so; I just find it hard to believe. Remember Pilate's lamentation to Jesus? "What is truth?" What some consider truth is very relative; while others are absolutely positive they know it all (at least more than anyone else).

There is another phenomenon that happens among us. We get the idea that since we've got a handle on truth, as we see it in one area, that we have a handle on it in others. I'm a big fan of Focus on the Family, for example. There are a lot of solid, inspired, and faithfully true teachings regarding the family and marriage in that ministry; however, that doesn't mean they are strong everywhere else in regards to church doctrines.

Some find certain preachers to be their favorite on the television, or radio, because they have learned so much. The problem is that we can become so enamored by one pastor that we'll swallow everything they teach: hook, line, and sinker. Can one person really have the corner on the market? Can one ministry be so deep that everything they teach, or believe, *is* gospel?

Paul admonished us not to become partial like this:

> "For when one says, 'I am of Paul,' and another, 'I am of Apollos,' are you not carnal? Who then is Paul, and who is Apollos, but ministers through whom you believed, as the Lord gave to each one? I planted, Apollos watered, but God gave the increase." (I Cor. 3:4-6)

We might not be saying I am of a particular person, but is there much difference in saying, "I'm Baptist," or "I'm Methodist," or "Catholic?" It helps us to understand in part where some of us are, to appreciate our backgrounds or current place in understanding faith, but doesn't it also hinder our walk as well? We do this in other ways when we proclaim this person's book, or that person's message or ministry, as great. I'm not condemning this practice; I'm trying to point out the difficulty we have in searching for truth. We become labels, we label others, and sectarianism is the result.

There is one more element that is the result of sectarianism. We can become fixed, dogmatic, self assured, cocky, even arrogant, and at the same time, determined to be right, defensive, threatened, protective, and argumentative. With this positional thinking, we cross over the ideas and concepts, *to attack the persons espousing them.* The idea isn't wrong, the person is. The concept isn't "idiotic," the one teaching it is.

Fellowship is lost and community cut off as each circles the wagons so to speak, to keep the others out. We set up camps, associations, and connections with those we see eye to eye with. We denounce or deny the authenticity and authority of those we disagree with. We have our banners, we have our codes, and we have our lines and recognitions of the acceptable and unacceptable teaching.

We have boxed ourselves in so that we don't compromise, pollute, or become tainted by heretics, the cults, and false teachers. I understand that we are to protect, guard, and be prepared to give a defense of our faith. I understand that we are to refute false teaching. My point is that we can become so threatened by others, we don't engage in discourse.

We are going to be surprised that many of our brethren, born of God (saved), have been in those *other* camps. Even cults have captured true children of God through their techniques and persuasion. How then does iron sharpen iron when we don't meet? When we don't engage, or talk to those who disagree with us? This means there is less fulfillment of helping each other learn, grow, and struggle through (as iron doesn't sharpen iron).

The tension can be caustic between us, because we removed it in our understanding of scripture. In a strange way, the tension is trying to balance us through each other. Most of the time, we're too carnal, or stubborn, or headstrong, to be brought back to the true tension coming to us from the Bible through those we disagree with.

At the same time, it can be difficult to engage in discussion with some we disagree with, because emotional barriers exist. "I just can't talk to so and so; I run into a roadblock." Or, "The dogmatic unbending, self assured cockiness, is unbearable!"

There is no give, no openness, and no dialog; it is just a one way street of superior thinking, or position on *their* part. There is no acknowledgment of possible self deception, no sense of possibly being wrong, and no appreciation that one could actually see it differently, and be Biblical. This difficulty with engaging with some may indicate the extreme left or right. Personal choices had been made to remove the tension so much that the rejection of it has hardened hearts.

The temptation for a child of God experienced in the Word, with years of study, who spends time in prayer, well traveled, exceptional mind and debater, is somewhere to cross a line that means he/she is no longer susceptible to error. We may have become so skilled at seeing the errors of others; we have become blind to our own.

It is as if growing in Christ means learning how to be right about everything. That maturity spiritually means having the right answers, having sound doctrine, being abreast of truth, as a person who has it together. My experience has been somewhat the opposite. The closer I walk with God, the more filled with the Spirit I am, the more I identify with Christ—the more wrong I have seen in me.

This may be a new challenge for some: if I haven't discovered *new* revelation where I thought *I was right*—something is wrong. I've been a Christian for over forty-six years, and I'm still waiting to arrive where instruction and reproof are not the way of life (of course I'm arguing that day will never arrive).

We are to teach and practice sound doctrine. That doesn't mean that we have arrived, and no longer need to be taught. Truth stands alone, and need not be attended by any one person— because God is truth. If a matter is truthful, whether or not we see it, defend it, *or think we own it,* is immaterial. The line that gets crossed is *ownership.*

We think we own the idea, concept, doctrine, teaching, or truth. What do we have that we didn't receive? And if we received it, why would we think we must defend it? It's God's truth, not ours.

And if it is God's truth, what makes us think we got it all? Do we all acknowledge Paul's teaching from the following verses, with emphasis added?

> "For we know *in part* and we prophesy *in part*."

And then,

> "*...for now we see in a mirror dimly*, but then face to face, *now I know in part*, but then I shall know just as I also am known." (I Cor. 13:9 & 12)

Somehow, we believe we know more than in part. Somehow, we see more than in a mirror dimly. We believe we know what we know, we are sure of it, we see it clearly, we are spiritual, and we are mature; yet, Paul, the apostle, who wrote much of the New Testament under the inspiration of the Holy Spirit, said this about himself too—the "we" included Paul.

A check and a guard: do we really believe we know in part? Do we really believe we see dimly? When we compare ourselves to others, we can become convinced that we know more, and see more clearly. Furthermore, we can cross over lines of tolerance and start declaring heresies of those who are basing what they believe in the Bible. We can cross over lines of respect for differences and declare others mishandling the Word of truth, because we *know* we are not mishandling it. It is ugly stuff when we are so certain, that we begin to put down others as false, erroneous, stupid, irrational, and accuse them of being deceivers—of practicing ill-will. We cross the line of loving others to judging them!

I can find myself emotionally charged when engaged in discourse, reading, or studying issues that I find hard to believe, or understand, especially if others *own the issue*. I can feel it tensing up within me. I'm threatened, and I'm bothered, sometimes angered, or bewildered why anyone would embrace such a view. The more I seek to grasp the other's position, the more uncomfortable I can feel.

It is a burden and a struggle; I'd rather not take it on. My reluctance is real, my personal pain, or anguish, is real; where does it come from? Is it pride? Is it insecurity? Is it iron sharpening iron (which I'm trying to avoid)? When we think of iron sharpening iron, wouldn't there be sparks? Wouldn't iron sharpening iron create much friction?

However, I'm comfortable where I am. I don't want to be bothered; besides the fact that I may have studied it before! I'd rather not experience the discomfort, and by removing it, I can find myself off to the left or to the right, thus avoiding the tension.

No one has all the truth. I remember being rebuffed by a brother in Christ, when in college, with those very words. I can still feel the dismay over thinking it through. I hadn't realized that my religious training led me to believe, or least act like, we did have *all* the truth. Our natural mind was convincing us that the way we saw it, is the way it was.

As I see the scriptures today, the more I think I know, the more I realize I don't. God is too much; I am grateful for the foundations and for the revelations that I hold onto now. Even so, I must keep from becoming closed about them. I still know in part, I still see dimly, and to claim that is all there is, is misguided.

Which brings me to what we can trust, what we can rely on, what I believe God placed in the scriptures to help us with this problem. The problem of our carnal nature dominating us to manifest in so much diversity, disagreement, arrogance and pride; influencing our decisions to cross over lines of truth to think we own our understandings, to cutting others off, of being threatened, or declaring superiority.

God knew we'd be in this malaise of human opinion and divergence—we are all so flawed (in our natural man). God knew that our sin nature would insidiously mislead us. God knew that our understandings of scripture would lead to fights, separations, and caustic behavior. What can we trust? What can we rely on? What is the help?

An answer: *God placed tension in scripture to keep us on the straight and narrow road, and off the broad wide roads of the left and right.*

# CHAPTER I

# THEOLOGY OF TENSION: AN ANSWER

The *Theology of Tension* simply means there are always two sides of the coin. There is always the left and the right of an issue. There are always two tensions pulling at each other. When one side is removed and the tension broken, that's when we get into real trouble.

## An Illustration of Tension

A crisis occurred back when Ronald Reagan was president. An American airliner was shot down flying over Russian air space. It had taken off from Alaska en route to Seoul, South Korea. The Russians claimed it was a spy plane and shot it down with over two hundred passengers aboard.

The reason I bring up this incident now is what happened to the airliner and why it was over Russian air space. Automatic pilot in those days, as it was explained to me, worked like this: a beam was broadcast from Alaska to Seoul and the plane's guidance system flew along that beam.

The plane doesn't remain on the beam perfectly. It will fly along until it detects the beam on its left, and then the guidance system will correct to fly closer to it. Then the plane may in time fly across the beam and find itself on the other side. The guidance system will detect the beam now on the right, and make corrections again to fly closer to it. This process will continue all the along the flight path, back and forth, left and then right. If the guidance system fails by removing the tension, the plane will drift to the left or to the right. In this case, the plane drifted way over to the right, flying over Russian air space, and was shot down for the reasons already mentioned.

I think this is a great way to understand the purpose of the tensions found in scripture. The tensions are created when scripture seemingly opposes, contradicts, or challenges our understanding, against itself.

On the one hand, the Bible teaches this; on the other hand, it appears to be teaching something different. What do we do with such things? The Divinity of Christ for example: there are passages that clearly indicate His divinity, and passages that clearly indicate His humanity. Many of us have struggled trying to figure out how both attributes can be true.

Many people, on the other hand, dismiss one or the other, removing the tension. Some have rewritten the Bible to remove this tension. If we keep the tension as God intended, we come to a place of seeing the God/Man of Jesus Christ: He was fully human and is fully divine. If we remove the tension, we will find ourselves off target, out in left or right field, missing God and the way to go in.

In truth, right now *all* of us are wrong in some areas of our believing, thinking, and teaching. We may not believe it about ourselves, but we certainly believe it about others. If it is true about others, then it is true about us.

We all should consider what we believe to be the place we are at now. This is with all of our good intentions, recognizing that we possess hearts that are deceitful and desperately wicked (in the natural). This is why scripture warns us *not* to lean on our own understanding (Pr. 3:5). We are pursuing the truth, seeking to be in God's will, and setting our eyes on Jesus.

The real work is of the Spirit, but we often succumb to carnal reasoning. To think that we've somehow arrived at *the* truth and have full understanding of any one teaching, issue, or area of life, is foolish.

I'm not saying that we can't know that we know from the Spirit what truth is.

This presents another area of tension. I can know I can experience the witness of the Spirit; the revelations of the truth bring faith, peace, rest, and joy. We certainly are to stand in these things, and at the same time, realize there is always more. The tension in the scriptures provides for our spiritual life and understanding to know; yet, at the same time, prevent us from becoming fixed, arrogant, cocky, and dogmatic. *The tension keeps us in the place of receptivity because there is always more!*

The following principle comes from experience in feeling the tension that scripture brings us to, if we remain faithful to the whole counsel of God's Word. These tensions can be found in Ecclesiastes 3:1-8:

To everything there is a season, a time for every purpose under heaven:

A time to be born, And a time to die;
A time to plant, And a time to pluck what is planted;
A time to kill, And a time to heal;
A time to break down, And a time to build up;
A time to weep, And a time to laugh;
A time to mourn, And a time to dance; A time to cast away stones, And a time to gather stones;
A time to embrace, And a time to refrain from embracing;
A time to gain, And a time to lose;
A time to keep, And a time to throw away;
A time to tear, And a time to sew;
A time to keep silence, And a time to speak;
A time to love, And a time to hate;
A time of war, And a time of peace.

## A Tool

Most of these issues are opposing each other. The scriptures contain many more examples, especially in the area of spiritual life and teaching. I share this principle that we should use as a tool. We should recognize the tensions, and then remain in them.

When we remove the tension in order to come to an answer, we have acted prematurely. In truth, our theology and beliefs will be *underdeveloped,* having short-circuited the work of the Holy Spirit to bring understanding and insight.

We will have jumped the gun, espousing our personal positions and dogmas—this, to me, is carnal reasoning. Let the tension remain; keep both sides as faithful, realizing that, when seen from the perspective of God's wisdom, they are invariably both true.

The question is how are both opposing issues true? Sometimes our human understanding will never grasp it; it is a spiritual answer from the Spirit life. The carnal mind wants to control it, bring it down to human concepts, when in reality the answer cannot be discerned except through the Spirit.

*The tension brings us to a point of being unable to make it work.* We must surrender to God's infinite wisdom *to receive* revelations of the truth. This place of surrender is holy ground, a sweet place to remain, a place of humility, and it prevents our carnal mind and pride from dominating us! This is how Jesus said He would build His church through revelation knowledge:

> "Jesus answered and said to him, 'Blessed are you, Simon Bar-Jonah, *for flesh and blood has not revealed this to you,* but My Father who is in heaven.'" (Mt 16:17 emphasis added)

## The Theology of Tension

The Bible has many tensions, and they exist because God placed them there to keep us on target. In the tension we are safe. It is also in the tension that understanding and revelations will come to us.

*By remaining in the tension, we are always acknowledging scripture.* We are affirming things even if we don't understand them. It keeps us safe from going to the left or the right on an issue.

In truth, it may be more than God just placing the tension in scripture; this is one way of looking at it. The other way is that for us to grasp the divine, it always produces tension in us, in our finite and human thinking. Since we are natural and carnal, being sense driven for most our lives, the practice of being spiritually minded competing with the natural, is going to produce tension just by seeing the divine.

Here are verses from scripture, with added emphasis, that reflect the tension and our need to stay within it:

> "Therefore you shall be careful to do as the LORD your God has commanded you; *you shall not turn aside to the right hand or to the left.*" (De 5:32)

> "So you shall not turn aside from any of the words which I command you this day, *to the right or the left,* to go after other gods to serve them." (De 28:14)

> "Only be strong and very courageous, that you may observe to do according to all the law which Moses My servant commanded you; *do not turn from it to the right hand or to the left,* that you may prosper wherever you go." (Jos 1:7)

> "Do not turn to *the right or the left;* Remove your foot from evil." (Pr 4:27)

The most outstanding is Jesus' teaching us about the narrow and straight path:

*"Enter by the narrow gate;* for wide *is* the gate and broad *is* the way that leads to destruction, and there are many who go in by it.

*Because narrow is the gate and difficult is* the way which leads to life, and there are few who find it." (Mt 7:13, 14. The NIV renders v. 14 as "But small is the gate and *narrow the road* that leads to life and only a few find it.")

The narrow road depicts a path that has broad and wide areas to the left and to the right, areas we do not want to walk in. The tensions found in scripture, seen as *contradictions,* are used by skeptics and other detractors to discredit the word of God. These *apparent* contradictions, in just about every case, have reasonable and sometimes awesome explanations. These explanations or revelations only come when the tension is embraced and both sides of the *apparent* contradictions are affirmed.

When the tension presents itself, we need to stay faithful to the messages; although to us they appear to be in opposition. We must ask the question in every case: "How can both of these passages that appear to contradict, oppose, or counter each other, be true?"

Fundamentally, we believe the Bible *is* the Word of God, meaning that we believe it is perfect, without errors, and faithful (in the original languages). Therefore, we must resist the temptation to relieve the tension by explaining it away, often by denying one side or the other. When we remove the tension, we have stopped the possibility of revelation knowledge coming to us. In essence, by choosing one side or the other, we begin to turn to the left or to the right and not stay on the straight and narrow.

In short, by removing the tension found in scripture we create tensions among ourselves by going to the left or right of understanding. If we remain in the tension found in scripture, we'll at least be closer to one another and have less tension between us.

Another by-product of removing the tension is that we can become "stuck." We will not progress in awareness and revelation *if we deny scripture.* This may explain how it is that someone with thirty years of experience, as a born again Christian, really hasn't grown much (at least in particular areas where the tension was removed).

Instead of becoming more aware and sensitive to the Spirit, their hearts have hardened and become somewhat blinded. The tension really is not only for our safety, it is for our good. It keeps us in the place of revelation and receiving, for the things of the Word of God are spiritually discerned. They are not matters of intellect, human reasoning, and deduction. The carnal man cannot receive the things of the Spirit (I Cor. 2:14)!

# CHAPTER II

# APPLYING IT: PREDESTINATION VERSUS FREE WILL

I want to begin to apply this *Theology of Tension* in the scripture in order to show, or demonstrate, how I see it working. I believe many denominations, sects, and separated churches of differing kinds, can somewhat be explained by how this tension is removed, ignored, and/or misapplied.

It is not necessarily the answer for all of our differences, but it helps to understand some of them. When the tension is removed, either to the left of an issue or to the right, we are certainly going to be on opposite ends in what we believe. Even when we apply the tension, I would guess that there would be a range of results continuing the differences; however, we will be closer to one another simply because we are all closer to the straight and narrow center.

When we do stay in the tension of scripture, this means that we are ultimately going to have to ask this question: "How do these seemly opposing verses both remain faithful to reveal who God is?" Or in other words, "How can these apparently contradicting verses both be true?"

## Predestination versus Free Will

The tension in scripture about these apparently opposing issues is tremendous. We find many scriptures that seem to express the complete sovereignty of God and many that seem to express man's dominion, responsibility and choice. There is no question that this tension has caused many to struggle with how *God's will interfaces with human will.*

If we remove the tension by declaring that God is sovereign completely, thereby, denying any significance to human influence or self determination, we will become ardent predestinates. If we remove God's sovereignty and control of human affairs by declaring that human will is what governs, and God is sidelined so to speak, then we become ardent as free will proponents. In truth, on both sides of this issue, there is truth being presented and ignored.

Here is a well known example of this tension in scripture regarding God's sovereignty as in predestination, and His mercy being predetermined; as opposed to free will, God loving all, and through Jesus, saving all.

> "As it is written, 'Jacob I have loved, but Esau I have hated.'" (Rom. 9:13; Mal 1:2, 3)

> "For He says to Moses, 'I will have mercy on whomever I will have mercy, and I will have compassion on whomever I will have compassion.'" (Ro 9:15; Ex 33:19)

"I will have mercy on those I will have mercy on..." declares God's own sovereignty and power. No one can oppose God; therefore, when we see verses like this one, we are very much tempted to see God has complete control, and *untouched by our human influence*—as if free will is not real.

Sometimes the Word of God simply shocks us with very bold statements like this one:

> "Then Jesus said to them, 'Most assuredly, I say to you, *unless you eat the flesh of the Son of Man and drink His blood,* you have no life in you.'" (Joh 6:53, emphasis added)

There are many other bold and attention getting verses that rock us to the core like when Jesus said,

> *"And if your right hand causes you to sin, cut it off* and cast it from you; for it is more profitable for you that one of your members perish, than for your whole body to be cast into hell".* (Mt 5:30, emphasis added)

No one is going to eat Jesus' flesh or drink His blood; neither is anyone actually going to cut their right hand off! This, of course, puts us in a bind that is impossible for us to get out of; we can't fulfill what is required.

These "shock" verses make us ask a question: "Is God testing us to see if we'll stay faithful to what we do know of Him?"

We know clearly that God loves everyone and has set before all of us dominion in the earth (John 3:16 & Gen. 1:24). It seems that the tension is a test, or at least a challenge for us, until the purpose of these opposing themes is revealed. When we choose one or the other to emphasize, we get into error. *We simply ignore revelation to run with revelation and it doesn't work very well.*

## "I Will Have Mercy On Those I Will Have Mercy On; Jacob I Loved, Esau I Have Hated."

When we take these verses on their own and remove the tension (from other verses), we are going to come out in one place; but if we keep the tension, we'll find our way to the truth and revelation knowledge of who God really is and how He set things up. To remove the tension (in this case) would be to totally discount free will, to stand in the place of God's complete sovereignty—meaning we have none (or very little).

At face value, in a very literal and singular interpretation, these verses are implying that God simply chooses whom He'll have mercy on, as if there really is nothing to base it on. It is describing God as already deciding as in predestining Jacob and

Esau's future. Many who embrace *Predestination* refer to these verses as proof.

If we let the whole counsel of God's word come together and *remain in tension* with it, we'll see something different.

For example, the following verses bring something to bear on the subject:

> "But from those who seemed to be something--whatever they were, it makes no difference to me; *God shows personal favoritism to no man*--for those who seemed to be something added nothing to me. (Ga 2:6, emphasis added)

And this fundamental truth:

> "I call heaven and earth as witnesses today against you, *that I have set before you life and death, blessing and cursing; therefore choose life that* both you and your descendants may live..." (De 30:19, emphasis added)

God shows mercy *without favoritism* and is no respecter of persons; yet this verse seems to say otherwise. God's word in many places sets life and death, blessing and cursing before us, subjecting it all *to* us (Deut. 30:19).

## Does God Predestine People's Future? Does God Decide To Love Some And Hate Others? Do We Really Have Choice?

Here is the answer that comes to me as we remain faithful to the tension this verse presents in light of others: God does predestine the righteous and the wicked in what they'll get and receive in judgment, both here on the earth and in the afterlife. It is in His laws of nature (the laws of this world), and the sowing and reaping process He put here (Gal. 6:7).

*"But the wicked will be cut off from the earth, and the* unfaithful will be uprooted from it." (Pr 2:22, emphasis added)

*"The curse of the LORD is on the house of the wicked,* But He blesses the home of the just." (Pr 3:33, emphasis added)

The key to unlock the confusion or conflict is to see it revolving around positions, not persons. If we look at the "wicked" as positions rather than persons, I think it all makes better sense. The "wicked" are those who do not repent, nor accept Jesus as their Lord. The end result of rejecting Christ is eternal condemnation. The wicked are those who decide to reject Christ; who do not become born again in the Spirit. Instead of turning to Christ and His gift of righteousness, they remain sinners without His grace.

The destiny and curse of life is upon wickedness, as destiny and blessing is upon righteousness. We get to decide which position we are in by what we do with Jesus.

## Video Game Analogy:

God's sovereignty can also be better understood by a video game analogy. The programmer programs the game, and within that game there are a multitude of choices and pre-programmed consequences. We could argue that the game is predestined in all its facets. If the game is pre-programmed, why would anyone play it? They play it because although they didn't have any say in the programming, they have lots of say about how they play the game itself. The controller gives them choice in a pre-programmed game.

Likewise, God's sovereignty programmed this world.

"Do not be deceived, God is not mocked; *for whatever a man sows, that he will also reap.*" (Ga 6:7, emphasis added)

Whatever a man sows means that we get to decide how we live our lives in God's world. The world, as we know it, has fallen from grace. It is sin cursed and will pass away. It is because of this, that the blessing of choices has become a trap, a curse, and bondage to us. Sin nature has caused us to use this gift badly.

## Is God Sovereign?

Absolutely God is sovereign; however, God *programmed choice* and gave us the right to it (that too is His sovereignty being expressed in our decisions). When human will is removed from the equation, and God's sovereignty is only understood by His complete control, a great misunderstanding emerges.

It means we believe that all of life and people's futures are all predetermined and predestined by God. It makes human free will just an illusion. We all know that the world is fallen and sin cursed as a result of human will; yet, somehow we just can't see God's sovereignty being diminished by our choices. God's sovereignty is manifest in and through our choices, just as the video game illustrates. The question isn't whether or not God is sovereign. *The question is how does that sovereignty of God work?* How did God in His sovereignty set things up?

## In Regards to Jacob and Esau

I reconcile that bold statement that God loves Jacob but hates Esau like this: the *positions* of wickedness and righteousness are determined. What is not determined is which one we'll choose.

*Jacob chose* in His life to prioritize the things of God, the birthright, and the firstborn blessing of their father. *Esau*, who was entitled to all those things, did not protect, value, or consider them *the* priority of his life. Their names became associated with those choices. God in foreknowledge knew the end and expressed it. That doesn't make God responsible for Jacob or Esau's choices.

God hates unrighteousness and wickedness; God hates sinner's selfishness and He is jealous for our good. There is no real good outside of God's will, purpose, and priorities in our life. We are to seek first the kingdom of God and His righteousness and all other things will be added to us (Matt. 6:33).

Esau sold his birthright for Lentil soup. Esau was not protective and ended up having his Father's blessing stolen by Jacob.

God hates the way *Esau valued things*; but we know God loves Esau personally because He sent Jesus to save him (John 3:16).

God loves Jacob as He loves everyone; therefore, this verse strongly points to the fact that God *loves the priorities of Jacob!* Jacob sought after, planned, meditated, and schemed to get the birthright and the firstborn blessing from their father. This kind of seeking, the desire after righteousness, is what God is after in all of us.

In other words: God is pleased with Jacob and displeased with Esau. God loved the way Jacob prioritized and hated the way Esau did.

God sent His Son to provide everything we need (what is not in Jesus?). What God has done for one, He has done for all; however, we must respond in faith to His awesome grace to receive Christ and the blessings in Him (Eph. 2:8). We must be established in grace: convinced, purposed, prioritized and focused, not distracted from it.

When we live to Jesus and prioritize the things of God first, we are acting like Jacob. When we lack desire, drive, and focus for His grace, we are acting like Esau. We are to accept, acknowledge and assert the things of God with authority: this overcomes our sin nature, the world, and evil (Philemon 1:6).

*It is the actions that God hates or loves* that are at the heart of this verse. It is not God determining whom He'll love personally. How do we know this? It is because we know other verses that say so: "For God so loved the world..." (John 3:16).

God is also saying that His mercy is not for sale, not for bribe, and not for earning. He shows mercy on whom He shows mercy based on who He is, not on who we are. God shows mercy on the humble, but resists the proud for example (Jam. 4:6); we get to decide to be humble or proud.

Anyone who comes to Christ receives forgiveness, *mercy*, and the gift of righteousness forever (Rom. 5:17)!

***Special Note:*** God's desire and interest in our lives is for us to seek first His kingdom, not for His immediate good, *but for ours!* God is blessed when we let Him bless us!

## The Conclusion:

God hates sin, but loves the sinner. God loves all of us the same in Christ Jesus. There is no way this verse should be used to communicate anything different about God, and it won't as long as we continue to embrace, affirm, and believe that all scripture is inspired by God for correction, reproof, and instruction in righteousness (2 Tim. 3:16). *When we keep in the tension that scripture creates*, it will keep us closer to the straight and narrow way. We may not have the understanding now, but if we affirm both sides of an issue revealed in the Word of God, we'll remain in a place where the Spirit can bring deeper understanding and revelation.

# Chapter III

# THE TRINITY: TENSION BEYOND COMPREHENSION

"Jesus said to them, 'Most assuredly, I say to you, before Abraham was, *I Am*.'" (Joh 8:58, emphasis added)

"You have heard Me say to you, 'I am going away and coming back to you.' If you loved Me, you would rejoice because I said, 'I am going to the Father,' *for My Father is greater than I*.'" (Joh 14:28, emphasis added)

There are so many verses we could use to illustrate the tension revealed in scripture about Jesus. I chose these because in the first verse Jesus identifies Himself as "I Am." This is clearly a statement by Him referring to the God of Moses, "I Am that I Am (Ex. 3:14)." He is literally saying, "I Am Jehovah."

Then in the second verse, Jesus speaks of the Father as greater than He is. This would place Him under God, a subordinate, a lesser class being, that He is not Jehovah.

If we look at only one side of the revelation, we'll come out with Jesus as a special being used by God to accomplish His salvation plan. We'd have to ignore so much other revelation to maintain this position.

If we remove the human side of Christ, and consider His incarnation purely divine, then we'll miss the substitutionary foundations of salvation itself (Phil. 2:5-7). Both sides of this incredible truth bring so much revelation of who God is and what He has made us through Christ (I John 4:17)! We'll miss a lot if we remove the tension to declare Jesus either divine or human, but not both.

**The definition of the Trinity**: The definition is sometimes the very thing that causes us difficulty in understanding the doctrine. *Tertullian* was an early Christian writer who lived in the second century, a scholar, and a tendentious debater of radical and uncompromising spirit of the faith. He evolved the earliest systematic form of the doctrine of the Trinity. He argued that there is one divine "substance" which is articulated or "administered" into three distinct but continuous "persons:" Father, Logos/Son, and Spirit.

At the same time, he offered a reflective account of the incarnation, explaining that the person of Christ is a union of two distinct, unconfused "substances," divine and human, in a single "person."

> 200 AD Tertullian "[God speaks in the plural 'Let us make man in our image'] because already there was attached to Him his Son, a second person, his own Word, and a third, the Spirit in the Word....one substance in three coherent persons. He was at once the Father, the Son, and the Spirit." (Against Praxeas, ch 12)

> 200 AD Tertullian "The origins of both his substances display him as man and as God: from the one, born, and from the other, not born" (The Flesh of Christ, 5:6 7).

This terminology became *the basis* of all later Latin and western Trinitarian and Christological discourse.

## All Is Based On the Interpretation of Jesus

Central to this doctrine and definition is *"The Interpretation of Jesus."* The trinity doctrine intersects with the incarnation;

furthermore, it builds upon the whole ministry of God sending His Son into the world to save sinners. Jesus is more than just a Savior to mankind; He is the focus for the whole of creation! All things were made by and through him, and for His pleasure they were created (Col.1:16). Jesus is more than just a divinely used human being: He is God, and as God, He is eternally significant in all ways like the Father and Spirit.

Jesus is the Logos (wisdom) of God made flesh, and being the Logos of God, He preexisted. He is divine and creative. Jesus said, "Before Abraham was, I am" (John 8:58). In Jesus, Spirit and flesh, divine and human, are one.

*The Trinity doctrine became necessary in order to affirm revelational truth.* The doctrine evolved in the Church through necessity to come against opposing views. It was not that the Church decided to have the "Godhead" of three distinct persons who are of one divine "substance;" the church was forced into articulating this doctrine by remaining in the tension that was revealed in scripture. The Church believed in One God; the Church believed in monotheism:

> *"Hear, O Israel: The Lord our God, the Lord is One!"*
> (Deut. 6:4, emphasis added)

*The problem is that strict monotheistic reasoning does not allow for Jesus to be divine: it removes the tension.* Furthermore, such restrictive interpretations of monotheism cause great difficulty with Jesus' new revelations. Much of what Jesus taught, and much of what the New Testament affirms, speaks to His divinity.

Is Jesus God? I have found over sixty-six citations in both the Old and New Testament sources that confirm this to be so (See website: Lordsbdt.com).

*What do we do with scripture that tells us one thing, but our monotheistic interpretations tell us another?* This is the tension that is found in the revelations written in both the Old and New Testaments.

This is the problem: first, we have a Savior who is a human being; second, we have this same human being making claims to His divinity; third, we are told that there is only one God.

## Is Jesus God? Was Jesus human? Was He both? Can He be God and God be in Heaven? Can God speak to God and still be One?

What we have are two undeniable truths: Jesus was human; second, that the scriptures affirm that He is divine. There is the tension!

## The Tension (Leads to Revelation):

To deny Jesus Christ is human is to deny the testimony found in scripture; To deny that Jesus Christ is divine is to deny the testimony found in scripture; To deny that God is One is to deny the testimony found in scripture; To deny that there are three distinct persons (Father, Son, and Holy Spirit) who are divine is to deny the testimony found in scripture; *To affirm them all is Christianity and the Trinity!*

To deny these truths at any point *is to make a human effort to relieve the tension.* The tension keeps us on the straight and narrow; preventing us from going to the left or the right; thus, missing the path and the truth (Duet. 17:20).

Here is *another analogy* that illustrates remaining in the tension that the Trinity brings, showing what the incarnation actually presents before us:

All games in life are *types of incarnations.* When we as human beings play any game with rules and limits, we are engaging in a similar activity that the Son of God engaged in when He became one of us. For example, *Monopoly* is a fairly well known game.

When we decide to play this game, we take on or enter into this game by "becoming" one of the moving pieces. We roll the dice and decide who goes first. We roll again and then move our piece according to the rules of the game.

We play fair when we obey the rules. We act in "supernatural" ways when we cheat. We have powers beyond the game rules and limits, but to play fair, we restrain ourselves and cooperate. That to me is the descriptive meaning of Philippians 2:5-8 (emphasis added):

> "Let this mind be in you which was also in Christ Jesus, who, being in the form of God, did not consider it robbery to be equal with God, but made Himself of no reputation, *taking the form of a bondservant, and coming in the likeness of men.*
>
> *And being found in appearance as a man,* He humbled Himself and became obedient to the point of death, even the death of the cross."

## The Trinity:

Let's not forget some fundamental truths in our understanding about God. One, God is eternal. Two, God is omnipresent. Three, God is omnipotent. There are attributes here that are infinite. How do we comprehend what is un-comprehendible? How do our finite minds, consciousnesses, and feelings grasp God? On the one hand, we do comprehend what God is, what God is like, and what God can do. On the other hand, we don't. Both of these things are true. We do and we don't comprehend the God we believe in—again, a tension.

> "Now to Him who is able to do exceedingly abundantly above all that we ask or think, *according to the power that works in us...*" (Eph 3:20, emphasis added)

We cannot comprehend the expanse of space, yet God is greater. We cannot look upon the Sun, and yet God is brighter still. We cannot count the sand of the shore, and yet God knows the number. We cannot think upon two things at once, yet God knows the thoughts of everyone at the same time. We cannot be in two places at once, yet we believe God is everywhere at the same time.

We have a beginning, a birth; yet, God has always been and will always be. We falter in trying to grasp these divine attributes. If we do not just accept them, we will drive ourselves crazy trying to understand them. In this sense, Jesus said we must be like a child. A child doesn't comprehend, but does accept—so must we.

The problem is that we want to understand and comprehend what we don't know; but how do we, finite beings as we are, understand God? It is easy to deny certain things sometimes, in order to put them in a controllable place. With the Trinity, people often deny its doctrine because they don't understand it, and want to place it in a controllable box. The danger can be in trying too hard to comprehend something, forcing an understanding. We make it be the way we want it to be or can understand it to be, this is the effort of the natural mind set; not the mind of Christ.

The struggle with the Trinity is whether we are dealing in *polytheism* or *monotheism*. Are we talking three Gods, or one? In our minds, in our perceptions, one is one being, one substance, and one *in* total. Three is three beings, three substances, or three *in total; yet,* there are many things created that do not fall into such simple terms.

## Examples:

-*Water* has three forms: ice, liquid, and gas. Does that mean water is one in three forms or three in three forms?

-*An apple* is one, yet there are three basic parts to its substance—peel, flesh, and core.

-*A human being is* one, yet we are a spirit, have a soul, and live in a body.

-*There are three dimensions*: height, width, and depth.

-*An* egg has *three* parts but is one: shell, white, and yoke.

## Conclusion:

The tension found in understanding and affirming the trinity is huge. If we remove one side or the other, we'll find ourselves missing the truth and grace found in Jesus. We'll become strict monotheists. This limits revelation. We may find ourselves in the camp of denying the deity of Christ. Remain in the tension, and we remain safe in the witness of the Spirit that Jesus is the God/man who came among us. Amen.

# CHAPTER IV

# THE CROSS IS THE ULTIMATE POINT OF TENSION!

There are many ways to explain the cross and Christ. I have chosen this one because *it illustrates the tension* that exists in the scriptures. When people want to know why Jesus died on the cross, we often give them answers that they generally cannot see for themselves. For example, we might say to such a question, "Well, He died to take away our sins!" This is the truth, but how does someone see this?

I have found an answer to that question that most of us can see and understand. In our world, we experience almost every day the tension I'm speaking of, and it points to the cross. *Furthermore, if genuinely understood, it separates the one true path to God from any other religion being offered.*

The tension I speak of in our world is the dynamics between *justice and mercy.* Here is the question, and then let me unpack what I mean:

> If God is just *and* God is merciful, how do justice and mercy find peace/satisfaction in a sinful person in relationship to God?

I think we find an un-resolvable conflict between them, concerning us before God's *holiness and mercy.*

*"He loves righteousness and justice; the earth is full of
the goodness of the LORD."* (Ps 33:5, emphasis added)

"The LORD is good to all, and *His tender mercies are
over all His works."* (Ps 145:9, emphasis added)

The scripture reveals that God is just and merciful. God loves
justice, and the earth is full of it. God loves tender mercies, and
they are over all His works. If we understand what justice is and
what mercy is, *there is a conflict and great tension.*

Simply put, *justice* defined is eye for eye, foot for foot, and life
for life—There is no *true* justice otherwise (Ex. 21:24. Further with,
"we reap what we've sown..." Gal. 6:7).

Simply put, *mercy* defined is that we don't get what we deserve
(We don't reap what we've sown). The tension is obvious, as mercy
*cancels out* justice and leaves it undone; then justice *cancels out*
mercy and leaves it undone (we can't have both!).

The question becomes: *"How can they both be satisfied in a
Holy God concerning us?"* The conflict is real if we affirm integrity,
honesty, and truth. If we let go, or remove the truth to "fudge"
or ignore reality, then the conflict may appear to be solved, but
Holiness is lost.

The only way we (human beings) can solve this dilemma is to
cheat. We'd simply forget to reap, or allow the circumstances to
pan out. In a way, it would be like throwing a rock into the water,
but there'd be no splash or ripples. We don't have cause and effect.

For God who is holy, just, and true, no such scenario exists.

"God is not a man, *that He should lie,* nor a son of man,
*that He should repent.* Has He said, and will He not do?
Or has He spoken, and will He not make it good?" (Nu
23:19, emphasis added)

In God's accounting, everything adds up and everything
reconciles. If we don't rationalize, justify, or play games, but look

intently at these two immutable attributes of God, we have a problem!

If we demand justice, or justice is satisfied, there is no mercy. If we demand mercy, or mercy is given, then justice is undone.

Look at real life situations: If someone *kills* another...*true* justice means the *killer* should be put to death (This is eye for eye, foot for foot, hand for hand, and life for life)!

If someone *cuts off* another's arm, *true* justice means the *offender's* arm should be cut off!

If mercy is granted to the murderer, then his/her life is spared. The murderer doesn't get what he/she deserves. If the one who cut off another's arm gets mercy, then this means his/her arm will not be cut off. Justice demands the arm be cut off. Mercy applied means neither the killer nor the offender (of cutting off a person's arm), get what they deserve.

In which case above will justice and mercy both be satisfied? How could both be satisfied?

When *true* justice is rendered, it really becomes a *lose/lose* situation: both people die; both people lose an arm. If *mercy* is given, one person lives and the other doesn't lose his/her arm, but both live with the fact that they destroyed *another's* life! (The victims receive no justice at all!)

*It is Christ in Christianity that solves the problem!* It is in the cross *justice* and *mercy* meet; righteousness and peace *kiss* each other!

> "*Mercy and truth have* met together; *Righteousness* and *peace* have kissed." (Psalms 85:10, emphasis added)

## In Satisfying Justice:

Jesus, the righteous Holy One, *substitutes* in our place. He *lays down His life for the world.* In dying, *Jesus satisfies God's holy judgment against sin* (What we sowed in sin, Jesus reaped on the cross in His death!).

## In Satisfying Mercy:

Jesus is raised from the dead, *"...because I live you shall live also!"* For anyone who calls upon the name of the Lord, there is mercy. Through the *blood of Christ,* God's wrath passes over us: we don't get what we deserve!

> And you, being dead in your trespasses and the uncircumcision of your flesh, He has made alive together with Him, having forgiven you all trespasses, *having wiped out the handwriting of requirements that was against us, which was contrary to us.*
> *And He has taken it out of the way, having nailed it to the cross.*
> Having disarmed principalities and powers, He made a public spectacle of them, triumphing over them in it. (Col. 2: 13, 14, 15, emphasis added)

Through the atonement, Jesus offers Himself for the sins of the world, fulfilling the law's requirements against us. Then, rising from the dead, He offers new life to anyone who comes to Him. Justice and mercy have met each other in the cross: in Christ, in Him. The *substitution works!* Justice and mercy have met together and found peace in God through the atoning blood of Jesus! The eternal tension between them is not removed by excluding one over the other; but both are satisfied, fulfilling the tension to bring us salvation! Amen.

What really matters is that God is satisfied!

## Conclusion:

*If you can find another way,* then what *Jesus* went through in being crucified would have been for nothing. He said, *"Father, if it is possible, let this cup pass from Me!"* (Matt. 26:39, He prayed it three times!) God, the Father, did not let the cup pass from Him.

*True justice* and mercy is something we can understand; and as we do *it points to the Cross!* No other religion satisfies this problem, and since Christ in Christianity does, it provides powerful understanding for why Jesus is the only way to God!

> "Jesus said to him, 'I am the way, the truth, and the life. *No one comes to the Father except through Me.*'" (John 14:6, emphasis added)

*The tension leads us to the born again experience*! Jesus answered and said to him, "Most assuredly, I say to you, unless one is *born again*, he cannot see the kingdom of God." (John 3:3, emphasis added)

# CHAPTER V

# PERFECTION VERSUS PROGRESSION

This tension has often caused confusion. The confusion makes us believe the wrong things. When we believe the wrong things, we'll miss God's grace. As born again Christians, are we new creations having been made complete in Him? Or, are we still sinners needing to press through to perfection in Christ?

Are we made righteous and cleansed from *all unrighteousness* as a gift (Rom. 5:17), or are we still bound and hindered by sin, so that we *must progress towards righteousness?* Are we forgiven of all our sins or just the sins we have confessed? The tension regarding our standing in Christ is quite debilitating for many because they feel guilt, shame, and constant defeat.

We often interpret our spiritual condition *based on how we're doing from our "old man" status* (This is an important point and needs to be unpacked). Then we seek hard to address our sin nature in order to clean it up. The more we appear to control the old man within us, the more righteous we feel. When we fall again, the disappointment can be devastating. What is going on?

Some describe this tension as moving on towards perfection in Christ. We need to grow spiritually from babes in Christ to mature Christians. The image that we see within us is someone that when born of God, begins as a baby would, like an infant. In time, with teaching and training, we progress from babies to toddlers, to little kids, to adolescents, to teenagers, to finally becoming adults. Even as adults, we see ourselves as young adults growing to full maturity becoming elders. All of this makes sense to our natural mind and what we see in our human experience. Is it what we find in scripture? There is tension in regards to this understanding. Let me begin to explain.

In I John we have this contradiction:

> *"Whoever has been born of God does not sin, for His seed remains in him; and he cannot sin,* because he has been born of God." (1Jo 3:9, emphasis added)

And from the same book, we have something that appears to be totally different:

> *"If we say that we have no sin,* we deceive ourselves, *and the truth is not in us.*
> If we confess our sins, He is faithful and just to forgive us our sins and to cleanse us from all unrighteousness.
> *If we say that we have not sinned,* we make Him a liar, *and His word is not in us."* (I Jo 1:8-10, emphasis added)

How can these scriptures both be true? One clearly affirms that the born again Christian *does not sin,* he/she cannot sin. The other clearly declares that we are deceiving ourselves *if we say we have no sin.* It goes onto say that we make God out to be a liar if we say we have not sinned. I think the tension is obvious and confusing.

Some reconcile this tension by ignoring it. Others present it as believers growing up in Christ spiritually, as in the physical sense already described. *I think the tension binds us from going to the left or the right as we affirm both are true.*

The answer, to me, is found in the dichotomy the scriptures present between the old man and the new:

"For the flesh lusts against the Spirit and the Spirit against the flesh; and these are contrary to one another, so that you do not do the things that you wish." (Ga 5:17)

We are born of God and have become a new creation, complete in Him (Col. 2:10), and this reality of the Spirit within us *does not sin*. It cannot sin, because it is born of the same divine nature as God (2 Pet. 1:4). Jesus and the Father have come to make their home in us because there is no sin in our new creation according to I John 3:9, and actually I John 1:9. I John 1:9 tells us plainly that as we confessed our sins when we became born again, the Spirit *cleansed us from "all" unrighteousness*. If we are cleansed from all unrighteousness, what is left? That would be consistent with this verse too:

"Therefore, if anyone is in Christ, he is a new creation; old things have passed away; *behold all things have become new.*" (2 Cor. 5: 17, emphasis added)

In our new creation spirit, we are just as Jesus is (I John 4:17). What I'm doing at this moment is presenting one side and substantiating it with other verses that agree. What I haven't done is remain in the tension by also affirming that we all have sin and commit it as Christians every day.

When we became born again, we didn't leave this body behind, nor did we lose the old man. Sin nature still dwells in our members. We are supposed to consider it dead (Rom. 6:2); however, as we all know, it is very much alive when it comes to our living life in this world. What this means is that when I sin, *it is not my new creation spirit sinning,* it is the old man taking opportunity within me. This is what I believe Paul lamented in this passage:

"But now, *it is no longer I who do it, but sin that dwells in me.*" (Ro 7:17, emphasis added)

And,

> "Now if I do what I will not to do, it is no longer I who do
> it, *but sin that dwells in me.*" (Ro 7:20, emphasis added)

We all struggle with this constant battle within us: either we live to the Spirit, or we default and live in our sin nature. We'll have this battle for the rest of our lives in this world. The victory, however, is not found in our efforts to put down our flesh. It is certainly not found in indulging it. It is found by living to the Spirit and His grace in our lives:

> "I say then: *walk in the Spirit, and you shall not fulfill the
> lust of the flesh.*" (Ga 5:16, emphasis added)

This tension is compounded sometimes by the way we walk in the Spirit. As babes in Christ, one could not walk, but would first have to be carried, then crawl, then toddle, and so on. This image of progressive growth can also be a hindrance. Are we progressing as in growing in our spirit, like we do in our physical body?

The scriptures are clear *that we are progressing. But* what kind of progressing is it?

> "*Not that I have already attained, or am already
> perfected*; but I press on, that I may lay hold of that for
> which Christ Jesus has also laid hold of me." (Php. 3:12,
> emphasis added)

How then can I be complete in Christ when I have not already attained? How can I be progressing toward perfection when in Christ I am made whole? How can both of these revelations be true?

Here are a few more verses regarding our perfection, emphasis added:

"For by one offering *He has perfected forever* those who are being sanctified." (Heb 10:14)

"But whoever keeps His word, *truly the love of God is perfected in him.* By this we know that we are in Him." (1Jo 2:5)

"No one has seen God at any time. If we love one another, God abides in us, *and His love has been perfected in us.*" (1Jo 4:12)

*"Love has been perfected among us in this:* that we may have boldness in the day of judgment; *because as He is, so are we in this world."* (1Jo 4:17)

The only way I see that both can be true is to see the separation within us as spirit, soul, and body. We have three areas of existence coexisting in our being. Furthermore, the bible describes the old man and our heart as battle grounds. Our heart, according to scripture, is where the issues of life are determined:

"Keep your heart with all diligence, *for out of it spring the issues of life."* (Pr 4:23, emphasis added)

Our new creation spirit is born again complete in Christ, having been perfected by His blood, cleansing us from all unrighteousness. The love of God has been poured out through our spirit, into our hearts (Rom. 5:5). This new creation spirit is not growing or progressing because "as He is, so are we in this world."

In our sin nature, we continue to sin. We continue to be selfish, willful, and rebellious, and do the things we don't want to do (Rom. 7). The problem is that we are not cleaning up the old man and making it better. There is no progression happening here. We are to consider it dead.

## Where Then Is Progression Occurring?

*We know clearly that progression is occurring from scripture.* We know that we are supposed to grow, but in what way? Is there growth and progression, or are we already perfected? There is the tension again.

> *"As newborn babies,* desire the pure milk of the word, *that you may grow thereby,"* (1Pe 2:2, emphasis added)

> *"But grow in the grace and knowledge of our Lord* and Savior Jesus Christ. To Him be the glory both now and forever. Amen.(2 Pe 3:18, emphasis added)

Growth occurs in two places specifically that I see: we grow *in our mind* by renewing it to conform to Christ (Rom. 12:1-3); and we *grow in our hearts* by the work of the Spirit (2 Cor. 3:18). In both cases, physical growth is not being described, *but growth in awareness and programming.*

This is a major understanding because spiritually we are growing aware of who we are in Christ—complete in Him. We are not growing in some capacity, size, or shape, in our spirit man. In our heart, where our dominion is expressed, we grow aware of, or in alignment with, God's word. Our hearts do not grow in capacity, size, or shape, like we did physically.

## Another Analogy: The Computer

When we buy a computer, it comes with stuff. Most come with preprogrammed software installed. We can add software as we choose, but for this simple illustration, let's assume that all of the software we're ever going to need comes with it already installed. When we bring it home as a new user, we need to grow in how to utilize it.

The computer doesn't grow in capacity or size; we grow in our understanding and ability to use it. What we are doing is becoming more aware, trained, and skilled, in how to use it. Likewise, when we became born again, we receive all that Christ is. The Father and the Holy Spirit dwell in us in the same capacity of Christ:

> "But if the Spirit of Him who raised Jesus from the dead dwells in you, He who raised Christ from the dead will also give life to your mortal bodies through His Spirit who dwells in you." (Ro 8:11, emphasis added)

And,

> "And of His fullness we have all received, and grace for grace." (Joh 1:16, emphasis added)

> "...which is His body, the fullness of Him who fills all in all." (Eph 1:23, emphasis added)

In reality then, our progression towards the things of God is not an increase in His presence, power, faith, life, peace, or rest. It is not an increase in capacity, size, or shape. If we have Christ, what don't we have? What we don't have is the same understanding, awareness, and confidence!

When we are established, certain, convinced, and filled with confidence, then we'll act boldly. We are like babes in our understanding of the things of God's grace. When we grow by the pure milk of the word, we are growing into understanding the perfection of Christ in us. So, because of the tension of perfection versus progression, when we come to affirm both, this leads to amazing revelations.

We don't have to consider that our sins are holding us back towards growth in perfection of Christ—we already are complete in Him. We don't have to consider that our addictions, habits, and weaknesses, mean that somehow we got less of Jesus. We have all received of His fullness and therefore, have all that we will ever have—it's already been given to us. *What are lacking are our understanding, awareness, and confidence.*

> *"As His divine power has given to us all things that pertain to life and godliness, through the knowledge of Him* who called us by glory and virtue, by which have been given to us exceedingly great and precious promises, *that through these you may be partakers of the divine nature,* having escaped the corruption that is in the world through lust." (2Pe 1:3, emphasis added)

As this passage affirms, we've already been given every blessing in Him. We are not progressing towards His righteousness. *We are progressing in it.* The confusion makes us miss His grace and our misunderstanding makes us weak in confidence to stand in the truth. We won't assert what belongs to us in Christ if we think we have to progress towards it as in some kind of merit-based growth (like in boys scouts working towards becoming an eagle scout).

> "...that the sharing of your *faith may become effective by the acknowledgment of every good thing which is in you in Christ Jesus."* (Philemon 1:6, emphasis added)

## Conclusion:

What God has done for one, He has done for all of us! We have all received of His fullness, grace for grace; therefore, acknowledge, assert, and stand in the truth. *As we progress in our awareness of His righteousness within us,* we'll experience the manifestation of His liberty in our lives. Our progression is about our awareness and application of His truth in our heart.

Our hearts and minds are the battle ground that must be renewed and changed in consistency. Our spirits are just like Christ, complete and perfect in the divine nature. As one might grow in their skills in using a computer, so we grow in skills in our new creation realities.

We are made perfect; yet, we progress in renewing our mind to think, act, and speak a new spiritual life, and plant the right seeds of growth in our hearts. Are we complete, or are we progressing in righteousness? The answer is both. A simple way of understanding this is: I am not working towards righteousness; I am working because of it! It is a gift given to me in Christ (Rom. 5:17.). Amen.

# CHAPTER VI

# SUFFERING: IS IT GOD'S WILL OR NOT?

This subject is much too involved and would require a book not a chapter; however, I present it briefly to provide *another major area of tension contained in the Bible*. At the core of this issue are two things: the *definition of God's will and one's understanding of it*. There really isn't any general disagreement *that Christians will suffer*. The controversy surrounds the *type of suffering* God wills for us to enter into, endure, and/or overcome.

What has happened is that tragedies, traumatic suffering, loss, devastation, and great grief, are sometimes blamed on God! For example, some people have been shipwrecked in their faith because they were told it was God's will that their loved one died. We even call huge weather events "Acts of God." There are better explanations that don't ignore the dominion of man, the intervention of Jesus, and the power of His name.

We get into serious error when we remove the tension and put forth terrible representations of who God is. If we believe that God is in control of everything and is the source for all suffering, then we are going to see a wrathful, mean, punishing, and even vindictive kind of God. If we think that God has no involvement, is disconnected, distant, and ultimately uncaring, we might turn away from the idea that there is a God at all.

These verses begin to reveal the tension, emphasis added:

"...for this is commendable, if because of conscience toward God *one endures grief, suffering wrongfully.*" (1Pe 2:19)

"For to you it has been granted on behalf of Christ, *not only to believe in Him, but also to suffer for His sake...*" (Php 1:29)

"For it is better, if it is the will of God, *to suffer for doing good than for doing evil.*" (1Pe 3:17)

Then, here are some verses that begin to speak otherwise, emphasis added:

"He *has delivered us from the power of darkness* and conveyed us into the kingdom of the Son of His love..." (Col 1:13)

"Who gave Himself for our sins, *that He might deliver us from this present evil age,* according to the will of our God and Father..." (Ga 1:4)

"*And the Lord will deliver me from every evil work* and preserve me for His heavenly kingdom. To Him be glory forever and ever. Amen!" (2Ti 4:18)

Two other major verses:

"...that I may know Him and the power of His resurrection **and the fellowship of His sufferings**, being conformed to His death..." (Php 3:10)

And Jesus taught us to pray,

"Your kingdom come; *Your will be done on earth as it is in heaven...* (In heaven there is no suffering)." (Mt 6:10)

The argument actually centers on the *kind of suffering* we are talking about. There are *sufferings from the fallen sin cursed world.* Many of these sufferings are listed in the curse of the law (Duet. 28). Then there are the *sufferings of Christ,* which we discover from His life and ministry and other books of the New Testament (Phil. 2:5-8). The distinction is critical and often overlooked. We come to understand and discern, to make the difference, by remaining in the tension the scriptures reveal in regards to suffering and God's will.

What are the true sources of suffering? If we are redeemed from the curse of the law, is that for now, or when we get to heaven? What does the life of Christ reveal? What about the lives of the apostles? What do the lives of Christians in general reveal?

## The Pitfall

Compounding this tension in a massive way is the phenomenon and **pitfall** that many of us make: *we interpret the scriptures based on our experiences.* When we do this, we are clouding the revelation and hindering our ability to see spiritually what is God's will. This pitfall takes us out of the realm of *biblical tension* and keeps us in the natural realm. We can't interpret spiritual things with natural or carnal thinking. We are to live by faith and not by sight (2 Cor. 5:7). When we allow experiences to dictate, dominate, and frame how we see the Word of God, we are living by sight. Hopefully, this verse is enough to validate this point:

> *"But the natural man does not receive the things of the Spirit of God,* for they are foolishness to him; *nor can he know them, because they are spiritually discerned."* (I Cor. 2:14, emphasis added)

The life of Christ is our example, and from His experiences, we do remain in the tension revealed in scripture. Because *He was sinless*, He didn't experience the curse of the law in His body—not until the cross. The apostles' lives are also good examples because they were the closest to Christ and commissioned to lay the foundation of our faith. The lives of the church in general, however, are mixed; going by the example of Christians as a whole will leave us all over the place.

To summarize, the issue isn't whether or not we are to suffer in this world, but rather which is the suffering that God expects and wills, and which is the suffering that is not His will?

If we accept all suffering as God's will, then we are removing the tension the testimony of scripture gives us on the new creation, the kingdom of God's grace, and the authority we've been given to address evil and the curse (James 4:7). If we say that God's people are completely delivered from all suffering in this world, then we are *removing the tension* by eliminating the testimony found in scripture in regards to the sufferings we're called to.

## All Things Work for Our Good?

Another aspect of the tension concerning suffering and God's will is God's amazing grace, mercy, kindness, and infinite ability to make everything work for our good! The problem is that although this is an awesome promise for all of us to embrace completely, *all things include the sufferings we're called to and the sufferings we're called out from.* The tension requires us to remain in the *Spirit of discernment*, so that we know which suffering to enter into and which we are to resist.

> "And we know that all things work together for good to those who love God, to those who are the called according to His purpose." (Ro 8:28)

## What about the Armor of God?

What is the point of putting on the armor of God if everything that comes our way is God's will, and we are to submit to it? If we don't stay in the tension, we are going to miss the grace of God in deliverance, protection, provision, and authority to overcome evil in this world.

> *"Put on the whole armor of God that you may be able to stand against the wiles of the devil."* (Eph 6:11, emphasis added)

> "Therefore take *up the whole armor of God that you may be able to withstand in the evil day,* and having done all, to stand." (Eph 6:13, emphasis added)

## Character through Suffering and Pain

Many believe and have been taught (or taught others) that without pain and suffering they would have never come to their senses. They would not have learned great lessons of sacrifice, hard work, endurance, and the victory of overcoming. Many have felt that their tough and painful experiences helped them to grow up, mature, and be more aware of other's suffering and pain. They became better people.

Some believe that without suffering and pain, we'd be weaker, immature, selfish, insensitive, and lack character. *Suffering and pain teach us hard life lessons that otherwise we'd never learn.* The sacrifices of parenthood, sacrifices of military service, wrestling with failure and success, experiencing winning and losing, not to overlook the suffering of self discipline in dedication, practice, long hours of study, and the denying of pleasures to seek a goal! All of these types of things have contributed to growth and understanding for many in life.

There is truth that we learn great lessons from suffering and pain; however, when we look at redemption, we must consider some amazing spiritual facts. When it comes to the *gospel of grace,* suffering and pain have taken on *divine purposes!*

The tension is that God does use all of our suffering, the good and the bad, for our good (Rom. 8:28). Our sin nature and selfishness often needs to be disciplined because of our lack of spiritual strength (the spirit is willing but the flesh is weak). When we get to heaven, for example, our sin nature will be removed entirely. We won't need to be buffeted, disciplined, or "suffer" in order to grow, develop, or have character.

We'll all be as Jesus is without the hindrance of sin nature (I John 3:2). We'll have His nature controlling us. We'll be obedient without issues. While we are here in this life, we must contend with the old nature. This is suffering we are called to (to deny the flesh):

> *"For the flesh lusts against the Spirit and the Spirit against the flesh; and these are contrary to one another,* so that you do not do the things that you wish." (Ga 5:17, emphasis added)

*Jesus suffered tremendously:* by being beaten, having His beard being plucked, a crown of thorns forced on His head, the thirty-nine stripes by the cat-of-nine tails with barbs that ripped open His back, the rejection of the people, the condemnation of the religious leaders, the betrayal of Judas and the abandonment of His disciples; then ultimately, the crucifixion itself was unimaginable pain, then finally crying out *"My God, My God why have you forsaken me?"* We know from the depiction found in Isaiah 53 that all of this suffering was a *substitutionary atonement for all of us!*

Listen to the verses again, emphasis added:

> "He is despised and rejected by men, A Man of sorrows and acquainted with grief.

And we hid, as it were, our faces from Him; He was despised, and we did not esteem Him.
*Surely He has borne our grief and carried our sorrows*; yet we esteemed Him stricken, Smitten by God, and afflicted. *But He was wounded for our transgressions, He was bruised for our iniquities; the chastisement for our peace was upon Him, and by His stripes we are healed.*"
(Isa. 53: 3-5)

Jesus' suffering and pain was not for Himself, but for us, to redeem us from sin and the curse of the law (Gal. 3:13). He bore our punishment, our judgment, and every claim of the law against us until God's righteousness was satisfied (Col. 2:13-15). The redeemer paid the price in full, and there is nothing we could ever do to contribute *one ounce to it.*

The suffering and pain that we experience now is often the consequence of our own decisions and/or those around us. It is from the fall and curse that is in the earth; however, as far as God is concerned, Jesus paid all of it for us—it is finished.

"These things I have spoken to you, that in Me you may have peace. *In the world you will have tribulation;* but be of good cheer, *I have overcome the world.*" (Joh 16:33, emphasis added)

The problem is that our sin nature is so dominant in our lives. Since we have learned obedience, discipline, and self control from the things we suffered (over and against our sin nature), *we want to attribute it as God's will for our lives.*

It is God's will for us to be separated from our sin nature. The new creation does this, but for God to give us our new glorified bodies where sin nature is completely removed, He'd have to take us from this world. This is to say that once we die, we won't need to suffer to learn things, grasp, or let go of selfishness, because we'll be just like Jesus in all His fullness (in our hearts and minds).

## There are Sufferings of the World
## and the Sufferings of Christ!

It is vitally important that we discern the difference so that we can walk in God's grace. Under grace, the suffering and pain we are to enter into now are the sufferings of Christ.

We learn from the life of Jesus the righteous sufferings He endured on the earth. The sufferings of Christ are: denying the flesh (Heb 12:4), resisting temptations, and obeying the law of faith (Rom. 1:5)! The suffering of fighting the good fight of faith to stay grace minded! To stay under God's authority and entrust all judgment to Him! Consider these verses:

> "For to this you were called, because Christ also suffered for us, *leaving us an example, that you should follow His steps:* Who committed no sin, nor was deceit found in His mouth"; who, when He was reviled, *did not revile in return;* when He suffered, *He did not threaten,* but committed Himself to Him who judges righteously; who Himself bore our sins in His own body on the tree, that we, having died to sins, might live for righteousness—by whose stripes you were healed." (I Pet. 2:21-24, emphasis added)

And,

> "Let this mind be in you, which was also in Christ Jesus: Who, being in the form of God, thought it not robbery to be equal with God: *But made himself of no reputation, and took upon him the form of a servant,* and was made in the likeness of men: And being found in fashion as a man, *he humbled himself, and became obedient* unto death, even the death of the cross." (Phil. 2:5, emphasis added)

The suffering and pain we experience as sons and daughters is to weep with those who weep, to sorrow with the lost and dying, to see the struggle and help the helpless. We must seek first the kingdom of God within us to be about the Father's business!

God's *will* is for us to walk as Jesus walked in this life (I John 2:6). His suffering was identifying with the lost. His suffering was seeing the great need. Therefore, He said:

> "Then He said to them, "The harvest truly is great, but the laborers are few; *therefore pray the Lord of the harvest to send out laborers into His harvest.*" (Lu 10:2, emphasis added)

The suffering and pain we experience under the curse of the law as Christians in this life misses grace. For Christ died to deliver us from it (we won't need deliverance from it in heaven—there is no curse there)! As sons and daughters, we are redeemed from sickness and disease because we have been *freed from the sin that caused it.*

> "For he who has died has been *freed from sin.*" (Ro 6:7, emphasis added)

There is suffering and pain that true Christians should experience: persecution, offenses (against us), trials, struggles, difficulties, hard times...that come against the truth in us.

> "Yes, and all who desire to live godly in Christ Jesus *will suffer persecution.*" (2 Ti 3:12, emphasis added)

## There Is Suffering that will be for our Good!

There is suffering and pain that we should rejoice in because it has come to us from doing what is righteous and good. It has come to us because we have fulfilled the call to walk in a worthy manner of Christ's calling (Eph. 4:1). As we live by faith in His grace, shining forth the love of God and sharing the gospel of Jesus Christ, the world will reject us. The enemy will place struggles, trials, and hard times in our way to discourage us. Just as it was with Paul, who had suffered many persecutions and difficulties on His missionary journeys, 2 Cor. 11:24-28:

> "From the Jews five times I received forty stripes minus one.
> Three times I was beaten with rods; once I was stoned; three times I was shipwrecked; a night and a day I have been in the deep; in journeys often, in perils of waters, in perils of robbers, in perils of my own countrymen, in perils of the Gentiles, in perils in the city, in perils in the wilderness, in perils in the sea, in perils among false brethren; in weariness and toil, in sleeplessness often, in hunger and thirst, in fasting often, in cold and nakedness—besides the other things, what comes upon me daily: my deep concern for all the churches."
> (2 Cor. 11: 24)

Certainly the love of God for the lost and dying is greater than His desire for us not to suffer pain, persecution, reproaches, rejection, distresses, and even needs. In fact, we should rejoice again that we are *counted worthy to suffer for Christ!* These kinds of sufferings, the sufferings of Christ, are good for us. When we avoid these things, resist them, and try to keep away from them, *we are missing God!* Indeed, for the love of others, God will lead us into these things as a by-product of witnessing for Jesus; but remember, this has with it a great reward in heaven (Matt. 5:12)!

Jesus said:

> *"If the world hates you, you know that it hated Me before it hated you."* (Joh 15:18, emphasis added)

> *"Therefore let those who suffer according to the will of God commit their souls to Him in doing good, as to a faithful Creator."* (1Pe 4:19, emphasis added)

We must discern between the sufferings of Christ and the sufferings of the world from the curse of the law! The world is fallen in sin and selfishness, and God's will is not being done on the earth. That is why Jesus said this:

> *"Woe to the world because of offenses!* For offenses must come, *but woe to that man by whom the offense comes!"* (Mt 18:7, emphasis added)

> "Then He said to the disciples, *"It is impossible that no offenses should come, but woe to him through whom they do come!"* (Lu 17:1, emphasis added)

## Conclusion:

Suffering and pain are a major part of this world. Many have suffered shipwreck in their faith because of traumatic and devastating suffering, wrongly believing that God is responsible. God is not the source of most of this world's suffering—it is caused by evil, people, and our own selfishness. When we remove the tension found in scripture concerning suffering, it will create confusion, divide us, and often make us weak in faith—even passive towards evil sources.

We must know the difference between what God's will is and what it is not regarding suffering. God's promise is to bring good out of evil and to make all things work for our good; however, that does not mean that all suffering and pain come from God! We need to stand in His grace to overcome the curse of the law and the deceptions of the evil ones. We need to embrace the fellowship of Christ's sufferings so that we can witness and reach the lost!

It really isn't whether or not we should suffer, but which kinds of suffering we are called to experience. It is remaining in the tension that is created by the scriptures: those passages declaring God's will that we will suffer and those declaring God's will that we are delivered from suffering. We must see the differences in suffering: the suffering of Christ versus the sufferings of this world. How can both themes regarding suffering be true? When we wrestle within this tension, we'll find answers. Some of which I have presented here. Amen.

# CHAPTER VII

# THE OLD VERSUS THE NEW COVENANT (THE LAW VERSUS GRACE); THE LAW DEMANDS BUT GRACE, IN THE SPIRIT, SUPPLIES!

The tension provided between the Old Testament and the New Testament is huge and often takes faith to even see it. The Old Testament is based on our efforts and is completely natural. In essence, if we do good things, we'll get good things; if we do bad things, we'll get bad things. The New Testament is based on Jesus' effort and is completely spiritual. Under the Old, we get what we deserve; under the new, we get what we believe.

The law demands, but the Spirit supplies. The law condemns, but the Spirit gives life. *The tension is everywhere!*

"...for the letter kills, but the Spirit gives life." (2 Cor. 3:6)

Consider these differences between the law of the Old Covenant and grace in the New Covenant. *They are not supplemental, or to be mixed.* Paul, the apostle, goes to great length to explain that the two covenants are completely different, and are based on *opposing themes* (the tension). The first is based upon our effort;

the second is based upon Christ's effort. The first is founded upon the law; the second is founded upon faith in God's grace.

> "Nevertheless what does the Scripture say?"*Cast out the bondwoman and her son, for the son of the bondwoman shall not be heir with the son of the freewoman.*" (Ga 4:30, emphasis added)

This verse, in context, refers to the symbols of the Old and New Covenants corresponding to Abraham's two sons, Ishmael and Isaac. Cast out the first to establish the second! They shall not be mixed, nor shall they remain together.

The works of righteousness from men that was based upon the standards of the law have completely failed; while *the gift of righteousness* has succeeded, providing salvation to all who believe! *God is giving to us what we could never have achieved through keeping the law.*

> "*Therefore it is of faith that it might be according to grace, so that the promise might be sure to all the seed,* not only to those who are of the law, but also to those who are of the faith of Abraham, who is the father of us all." (Ro 4:16, emphasis added)

## Examine These Differences:

The law requires our compliance to the *smallest detail*; it demands righteousness. Grace, through the Spirit, forgives and saves us to the *smallest detail*, through the blood of Christ.

> "'Cursed is the one who does not confirm *all the words of this law* by observing them.' And all the people shall say, 'Amen!'" (De 27:26, emphasis added)

> "Therefore He is also able *to save to the uttermost* those who come to God through Him, since He always

lives to make intercession for them." (Heb 7:25, emphasis added)

The law curses anyone who cannot keep any part of it; by no means will the law overlook sin: the soul that sins shall die. The Spirit blesses anyone who can *believe in the believing one,* even as small as a mustard seed; grace gives forgiveness of sins in Christ's blood—the gift of righteousness.

"For whoever shall keep the whole law, and yet stumble in one point, *he is guilty of all."* J(as 2:10, emphasis added)

"There is therefore *now no condemnation to those who are in Christ Jesus,* who do not walk according to the flesh, but according to the Spirit." (Ro 8:1, emphasis added)

The law examines us and condemns even the best of us; the law keeps a record of wrongs. Grace through the Spirit in Jesus, saves even the worst of us and atones for all sin, forever! Grace separates our sins from us as far as the East is from the West.

"*But that no one is justified by the law* in the sight of God is evident, for "the just shall live by faith." (Ga 3:11, emphasis added)

"*For by grace you have been saved through faith,* and that not of yourselves; it is the gift of God..." (Eph 2:8, emphasis added)

"For by one offering He *has perfected forever* those who are being sanctified." (Heb 10:14, emphasis added)

"As far as the east is from the west, So far has He removed our transgressions from us." (Ps 103:12)

The law burdens us with responsibility, always reminding us that we are falling short, and that we are law breakers; it prosecutes us and pronounces, "You shall not..." Grace through the Spirit, carries us and always reminds us that *Christ is our righteousness*, and we are new creations; the old is past, and we are now sons and daughters of God.

> "...*for if the ministry of condemnation (the law)* had glory, the ministry of righteousness exceeds much more in glory." (2Co 3:9, emphasis added)

> "Now we know that whatever the law says, it says to those who are under the law, that every mouth may be stopped, *and all the world may become guilty before God."* (Ro 3:19, emphasis added)

> "For if by the one man's offense death reigned through the one, *much more those who receive abundance of grace and of the gift of righteousness* will reign in life through the One, Jesus Christ." (Ro 5:17, emphasis added)

> "Therefore, if anyone is in Christ, *he is a new creation*; old things have passed away; behold all things have become new." (2 Cor. 5: 17, emphasis added)

Under the law we are in bondage to sin, *held captive by the power of it* (I Cor. 15:57). Under grace and the Spirit, we are set free in the *liberty of Christ,* and supplied the power of God to walk in *newness of life.*

> "The sting of death is sin; *and the strength of sin is the law."* (I Cor. 15:56, emphasis added)

> "*But now we have been delivered from the law,* having died to what we were held by, so *that we should serve in the newness of the Spirit* and not in the oldness of the letter." (Ro 7:6, emphasis added)

Under the law, we were provoked, prodded, convicted, oppressed in guilt and shame. Under grace, we are empowered, prompted, and *supplied* freedom to love God *by His love for us.*

> "...and release those who through *fear of death were all their lifetime subject to bondage.*" (Heb 2:15, emphasis added)

> "Stand fast therefore in the *liberty by which Christ has made us free,* and do not be entangled again with *a yoke of bondage.*" (Ga 5:1, emphasis added)

Under the law, we *related to regulations,* statues, and dos and don'ts. Under grace, *we relate to Jesus.* We see Him in His glory in us, and by the Spirit, we are *transformed into the same image;* we relate to the peace and the joy of the Lord in His pleasure.

> "Tell me, you who desire to be under the law, *do you not hear the law?*" (Ga 4:21, emphasis added)

> "But we all, with unveiled face, *beholding as in a mirror the glory of the Lord,* are being *transformed into the same image from glory to glory,* just as by the Spirit of the Lord." (2Co 3:18, emphasis added)

Under the law, we are constantly reminded of our sin; we are sin conscious. Under grace, we are constantly reminded of our acceptance in the beloved; *we are Christ conscious!*

> "...for all have sinned and *fall short of the glory of God,*" (Ro 3:23, emphasis added)

> "And when He (Holy Spirit) has come, *He will convict the world of sin, and of righteousness,* and of judgment..." (Joh 16:8, emphasis added)

Under the law, we labored *for* God's blessings. Under grace, we labor *with and because of* God's blessings

> "The LORD your God will make you abound in all the work of your hand, in the fruit of your body, in the increase of your livestock, and in the produce of your land for good.
> For the LORD will again rejoice over you for good as He rejoiced over your fathers, *if you obey the voice of the LORD your God, to keep His commandments* and His statutes which are written in this Book of the Law, and if you turn to the LORD your God with all your heart and with all your soul." (Deut. 30: 9, 10, emphasis added)

> "...as His divine power *has given to us all things* that pertain to life and godliness, *through the knowledge of Him who called us by glory and virtue...*" (2Pe 1:3, emphasis added)

Under law, we are heavy laden (in constant battle), on our own, with no peace, and no rest for our souls. Under grace, we are *yoked with Christ,* who gives us His strength and peace. He never leaves us nor forsakes us, and we find rest for our souls.

> "Now therefore, why do you test God by *putting a yoke on the neck of the disciples* which neither our fathers nor we were able to bear (keeping the law)?" (Acts. 15: 10, emphasis added)

> "Come to Me, all you who labor and are heavy laden, *and I will give you rest.*
> "*Take My yoke upon you* and learn from Me, for I am gentle and lowly in heart, and you will find rest for your souls. "For My yoke is easy and My burden is light." (Matt. 11: 28-30, emphasis added)

"Peace I leave with you, *My peace I give to you*; not as the world gives do I give to you. Let not your heart be troubled, neither let it be afraid." (Joh 14:27, emphasis added)

Under law is the *knowledge of sin*. Under grace and the Spirit, *is the knowledge of Christ!*

"Therefore by the deeds of the law no flesh will be justified in His sight, *for by the law is the knowledge of sin.*" (Ro 3:20, emphasis added)

"...*that I may know Him* and the power of His resurrection, and the fellowship of His sufferings, being conformed to His death," (Php 3:10, emphasis added)

Under law, we were dead in trespasses and sins, being separated from the love of God. Under grace, we are made alive and brought new life in Jesus, *to know God's love!*

"But God, who is rich in mercy, because of His great love with which He loved us, *even when we were dead in trespasses, made us alive together with Christ* (by grace you have been saved)..." (Eph 2:4, 5, emphasis added)

"...*to know the love of Christ* which passes knowledge; that you may be filled with all the fullness of God." (Eph 3:19, emphasis added

"...till we all come to the *unity of the faith and of the knowledge of the Son of God,* to a perfect man, to the measure of the stature of the fullness of Christ;..." (Eph 4:13, emphasis added)

The law demands, but we are bankrupt! On our own, we do not have the resources, or the love of God in us, to measure up or be counted worthy. The law is for sinners: it is natural, and it is not of faith (Gal. 3:12). *Grace is for the saints: it is supernatural and it is full of faith.*

## The Spirit Supplies and Provides Abundant Grace in Christ Jesus!

Many of us have held onto the law, especially the Ten Commandments; however, the law makes no one perfect (Heb. 7:19)! As long as we hold onto it, remain governed by it, we are missing out on the power of our salvation.

Salvation is not found in keeping the law, for no one could do it. Jesus came and fulfilled the law. He did away with it, making it *unnecessary* in our lives when we come to Him (Heb. 8:13). Now we have this vast spiritual life born into us, based not on relating to the law, but totally relating to Jesus and His grace!

The law limits our ability to see Jesus; in fact, it veils our eyes (2 Cor. 3:16)! It is when we see the abundant life in Him, through the new creation that we are genuinely set free!

The tension comes because in our natural man we can't see His grace, and we are bound by naturalism. Under grace, we are joined with the Lord and live to His supernatural truth within us.

## In Conclusion

As we understand the differences between the Old and New Covenants, we can begin to discern and sift out the law in our life. When we live to the law, we are living in the flesh (I Tim. 1:9). When we live to the law, we are estranging ourselves from Christ and grace profits us nothing (Gal. 5:1-4). When we examine and focus on grace, we see a whole new world.

This newness of life restored our relationship to God, based upon His love, His gifts, His mercy, and His supply! From the very beginning, God has always meant to be our source, our supply, and our sustainer. We are responders to His grace! As we look further, we see awesome things in creation, in relationships, and especially in His Word, that show us how deep, how long, how wide, and how fully God loves us!

Now that we are born again, we have been joined to this abundant life in Jesus. We are connected to the unlimited One. The Old Covenant was weak because we couldn't keep it. The law was given to expose this truth and point to the New Covenant. The New replaces the Old, and completely supersedes it. When Jesus spoke about new wine needing new wine skins, that has everything to do with the new creation and living in the Spirit; the old wine skins and old wine are no longer needed (Matt. 9:17). The old nature and the Old covenant, including the law, have become *obsolete*:

> "In that He says, 'A new covenant,' *He has made the first obsolete.*
> Now what is becoming obsolete and growing old is ready to vanish away." (Heb 8:13, emphasis added)

The tension that God's law from the Old Testament puts on us is unbearable. We cannot love God with all our heart, or our neighbor as ourselves. We fall far short of keeping the Ten Commandments; all of it points to our need for the savior.

When we try as born again believers to keep the law as best we can, we become sin conscious again; this brings us back under the curse. The answer is our relationship, not to the law, but to Jesus Himself (2 Cor. 3:18)!

He is our intercessor and mediator, who fulfilled the law's demands against us (Col. 2:13, 14). We now relate fully to the Lord, through newness of life. We are translated from the kingdom of darkness (the world), into the kingdom of His dear Son (Col. 1:13)! We've gone from the burden being upon us, to being carried in His grace always. The burden was upon Him; He finished the race and won the victory. He now turns to us and gives us what was His, while taking away what was ours. Amen.

***Special Note:*** The tension between the Old and New Covenants is huge, as I've tried to explain; however, the whole idea of putting away the law and just living to Christ, creates a whole other area of tension. Many, upon hearing this, immediately respond as Paul wrote:

> "What shall we say then? *Shall we continue in sin that grace may abound?" (*Ro 6:1, emphasis added)

I'm not taking the time in this chapter to address and unpack this tension. Let me leave it by saying: "Grace, in Christ, through Christ, in His Spirit, will never lead us into sin; quite to the contrary, it will empower us out of it."

Maybe a final illustration will help capsulate it? I have two dogs that need no fence. We let them out every day into our yard (staying within it). They do their business and return to the front door always. Many dogs need a fence because if they are let out, they will run.

The fence represents the *Law of Moses* in our lives. It was there to constrain us from becoming utterly depraved (As in the days of Noah before the flood). At the same time, it exposed our sins, pointing us to Jesus (Gal. 3:24). When we come to Christ, who is our life, strength, peace, and rest, we stop running! We are new creations in Him, and we don't need the fence anymore (2 Cor. 5:17)!

# CHAPTER VIII

# WAITING: ARE WE WAITING UPON THE LORD OR IS HE WAITING UPON US?

*"Wait on the LORD;* be of good courage, And He shall strengthen your heart; *Wait, I say, on the LORD!"* (Ps 27:14, emphasis added)

*"But those who wait on the LORD shall renew their strength;* they shall mount up with wings like eagles, they shall run and not be weary, they shall walk and not faint." (Isa 40:31, emphasis added)

*"Rest in the LORD, and wait patiently for Him;* Do not fret because of him who prospers in his way, Because of the man who brings wicked schemes to pass." (Ps 37:7, emphasis added)

There is a strong understanding from the Old Testament of our need to wait upon the Lord. We are to wait for the Lord's intervention and salvation. We must not go ahead of Him, but wait for His timing. In His time, God will move. In His time, God will answer. In His time, all things will work for our good (Rom. 8:28).

Now, consider some of these verses from the New Testament that share something quite different, emphasis added:

*"Put on the whole armor of God that* you may be able to stand against the wiles of the devil." (Eph 6:11)

"For you were once darkness, but now you are light in the Lord. *Walk as children of light...*" (Eph 5:8)

"For this reason we also, since the day we heard it, do not cease to pray for you, and to ask that you may *be filled with the knowledge of His will in all wisdom and spiritual understanding; that you may walk worthy of the Lord, fully pleasing Him, being fruitful in every good work* and increasing in the knowledge of God;..." (Col 1:9, 10)

Things have changed since the atonement! Under the Old Testament, we are to wait for God to move. We were waiting for God's salvation; however, in the New Testament, *we are no longer waiting.* Under the New Testament, we are to put on Christ! We are to walk as Christ walked in the light of God's will. We are to be filled with the knowledge of His will in all wisdom and spiritual understanding (Col. 1:9). We are to be filled with the Spirit (Eph. 5:18). We are to walk worthy of the Lord, fully pleasing Him (Col. 1:10). All of these things point to a new day that the Lord has made. In this new day, grace has moved, accomplished, and fulfilled salvation—it is finished (John 19:30).

So, which is it now? *Do we wait upon the Lord, or is the Lord waiting on us?* When we experience the New Testament phenomenon of the new birth, but maintain an Old Testament mindset, we are missing something. We are to renew our minds to conform to the will of God (Rom. 12:1-3). The Old Testament has been updated by the most important event in human history—*the crucifixion of Christ!*

Under the Old Covenant, we were waiting on God's power, presence, deliverance, and redemption. Under the New Covenant, these things have already been provided in His grace through the cross. All of these things have now become subject to us. That is an incredible truth!

> *"Go therefore and make disciples of all the nations,* baptizing them in the name of the Father and of the Son and of the Holy Spirit..." (Mt 28:19, emphasis added)

> "But you shall receive power when the Holy Spirit has come upon you; and *you shall be witnesses to Me* in Jerusalem, and in all Judea and Samaria, and to the end of the earth." (Ac 1:8, emphasis added)

> "And the spirits of the prophets *are subject to the prophets.* (1Co 14:32, emphasis added)

God is now waiting on us! He is waiting on us to believe, to be established in grace (Heb. 13:9), and to work the works of Christ through His power (John 14:12). The following statement becomes true, if we affirm both sides of the tension in regards to waiting: *God isn't the one who determines when His blessings are manifested.*

When we wait upon the Lord, as in the Old Testament situation, we are waiting for Him to move (as if He hasn't)! When we wait upon the Lord as in the New Testament situation, we are only waiting for Him to fulfill promises not yet kept (i.e. the rapture, the second coming, and our new glorified bodies).

What about salvation? What about the atonement? What was finished when Jesus said, "It is finished?" What God did in Jesus, fulfilled the law, took away our sin, brought us peace and rest, and established us in Christ as new creations. What is the new creation? What has grace already given us, as Peter wrote?

> "...as His divine power *has given to us all things that pertain to life and godliness,* through the knowledge of Him who called us by glory and virtue..." (2Pe 1:3, emphasis added)

What more can God do than give us Jesus? Therefore, it isn't up to God when we get saved, healed, provided for, protected, or experience His presence since the cross. *This has been and is a major stumbling block for the body of Christ. We keep waiting on God from an Old Testament mindset, when this is the day of salvation!*

If one believes that we are waiting on God in His timing, in His sovereignty to move and manifest these things (all that is in salvation), we are going *to wait a long time*, because *God is waiting on us to use what He's already provided.*

There is a large part of the body of Christ who believe that God's sovereignty means that we are *not* responsible, and that all things depend upon God's timing. We sing songs about God moving in His time, we say prayers declaring the same things; we comfort each other assuring that things will be okay in "His time."

We may think waiting on God's timing is humility, obedience, patience, and perseverance (It was under the Old Covenant); however, *"Today is the day of salvation,"* do not harden your hearts it says, as in the days of the rebellion, when the children of Israel refused to believe God and God had to turn them back into the wilderness (Heb. 3:15). *Today is now*, for God has moved, and we don't need to wait on Him and salvation any more.

## What Does God's Sovereignty Mean?

The scripture says, "God is not mocked whatsoever a man sows that shall he also reap (Gal. 6:7)." We get to decide what we'll sow, but we don't get to decide what we'll reap, that is the part that is predetermined. If I plant corn, I don't get to decide I want gold coming up in the kernels. If I plant apples, I don't get to decide I want a money tree. God's sovereignty means that it is *the laws* that are the power behind life (I Cor. 15:57). God is His laws, and they operate whether we like them, know about them, or try to fight against them!

God's rule means that we are under the curse of the law and stand in condemnation because we are sinners (John 3:18); but that isn't the end of the story. God's grace and mercy has been extended to us through the cross, so that we don't get what we deserve; we can get what we believe in Jesus (Gal. 3:13).

We all believe in predestination in the sense that life has rules programmed into it. Like a computer game, the programmer has programmed everything, including all the choices a game player can make. Predetermined are all the *available choices* and their results, and then the controllers are given to us.

Why would anyone want to play a video game? All of it is predetermined; yet many play and become obsessed with playing. This is because the choices are so varied and mimic life possibilities. Players forget it's all planned because they can choose which plan or path to take.

## Wait Upon the Lord?

> "For evildoers shall be cut off; *But those who wait on the LORD, They shall inherit the earth.*" (Ps 37:9, emphasis added)

*Before the cross of Christ,* the whole earth was waiting on the Lord's salvation. They had to wait until the day of salvation, but *we don't.* That day is upon us! Listen again:

> "For He says: *"In an acceptable time I have heard you,* And in the day of salvation **I have helped you."** Behold, *now* is the accepted time; behold, *now* is the day of salvation." (2Co 6:2, emphasis added)

Under the Old covenant this was the situation:

> "I call heaven and earth as witnesses today against you, *that I have set before you life and death, blessing and cursing; therefore choose life that both you and your descendants may live...*" (De 30:19, emphasis added)

God set before us life and death, blessing and cursing. All of this was under the law and on us. This all changed, for the promised savior has come and delivered us from the curse of the law (Gal.3:13). Today is the day of salvation, based completely on what God did. There is no more waiting for God to move to bring salvation to us!

God has already decided, as far as He is concerned, that in Christ we are blessed, provided for, and healed; we are His children and joined as one with the Lord (I Cor. 6:17). Anytime we want to approach God in prayer we have access—God is not the one who determines when we pray. Anytime we want to spend time in God's presence and experience more of Him, we have access through the Blood through forgiveness of sins. God is not the one who determines when, who, why, or where, we experience His presence. God *has* determined how and through whom we pray—that is in Jesus, the Word of God through His Spirit; however, when we pray is up to us.

*This is huge; this is major!* We've gotten the idea that we must blast heaven with tears, begging, bringing continual requests to make God *move*, to touch us, and to provide for us. We do this because we have an *Old Testament* mindset that is still waiting on God to move, as if He hasn't yet. He moved in Christ! It must really try His patience when we continually ask for Him to do what He's already done.

## Consider Our Salvation

Jesus died two thousand years ago, and when He was on the cross He said, *"It is finished."* Salvation is complete and anyone who calls upon the name of the Lord shall be saved (Rom. 10:13). The time, God's timing, *is now!* It has been now ever since Jesus rose from the dead. *This is the acceptable time!* This is the time to make our claim, today, *as long as it is still called today,* anyone can be saved; but who determines when? We do.

It is already decided on God's part to save. The payment is paid in full. The costs are already covered. What takes place next, God doesn't control. When a sinner repents there is great joy by the Father in heaven in the presence of the angels. Why? It is because God in His sovereignty established that each soul will choose.

When a sinner repents, it is God's *initiative*, but it is his or her free response that brings joy to the Father. What a strange paradox: no one can come to the Father unless the Spirit draws him/her; however, it is not until the sinner repents in Jesus' name that salvation begins.

**Here are New Testament Verses Dealing with "Waiting,** with emphasis added:**"**

> "But if we hope for what we do not see, *we eagerly wait for it with perseverance.*" (Ro 8:25)

> "Therefore, my brethren, when you come together to eat, *wait for one another.*" (1Co 11:33)

> "For we through the Spirit *eagerly wait for the hope of righteousness by faith.*" (Ga 5:5)

> "For our citizenship is in heaven, *from which we also eagerly wait for the Savior,* the Lord Jesus Christ..." (Php 3:20)

> "*...and to wait for His Son from heaven,* whom He raised from the dead, even Jesus who delivers us from the wrath to come." (1Th 1:10)

> "...so Christ was offered once to bear the sins of many. *To those who eagerly wait for Him He will appear a second time, apart from sin, for salvation.*" (Heb 9:28)

Some of this *waiting* has to do with promises that God has not yet fulfilled: the second coming, our receiving resurrected glorified bodies, the new heaven and earth, and for God's kingdom to be fully realized upon the earth. Furthermore, we are to wait for one another patiently, serving, helping, encouraging, and providing strength and grace in weakness.

We are to wait as in *declaring a thing (Mark 11:23)* and expecting like a woman waiting to bear a child. We wait to see what we have already put into motion by the authority given to us in Christ. We wait eagerly, not for God to move, but for the situation, circumstances, and symptoms to move! We wait to see those we prayed for in healing to recover (Mark 16:18)!

This waiting is different than the waiting we were supposed to do before the atonement and becoming born again. The tension is caused because we can clearly see the admonitions to wait for God's timing from the Old Testament scriptures; then we see from the New Testament, a new place or position given to us in Christ.

In the old situation, we needed to wait for God to move because Christ had not yet been glorified. Now in the new, God has moved: we must wait for the power within us to move the circumstances, situations, symptoms, and cursed realities to align with God's will that we put into motion!

> "Now to Him who is able to do exceedingly abundantly above all that we ask or think, *according to the power that works in us...*" (Eph 3:20, emphasis added)

Before the cross and under the law, Jesus said that everything was, *"be it unto you according to your faith* (Mark 9:29)." That put the burden upon us to believe God and exercise faith. We were all in trouble, because we could not keep the law and our faith was very little; furthermore, our faith did not have the grace and love of God poured out into our hearts because the new birth was not available (Rom. 5:5). One of the fruits of the Holy Spirit to us is faith (Gal. 5:22 *AV*)! Now, in the new creation realities, everything is according to the power of God's presence, life, and Spirit, through Christ, within us. It all depends upon our relationship to Jesus:

"But we all, with unveiled face, *beholding as in a mirror the glory of the Lord, are being transformed into the same image from glory to glory,* just as by the Spirit of the Lord." (2 Cor. 3:18, emphasis added)

## Guess Who Decides Who Walks After the Spirit, to Behold the Lord?

God does not determine this, we do! The promises of God are all subject to us. When it comes to spiritual life: will we stand, assert, and walk by the Spirit? Who decides this? We do.

"For *all the promises of God in Him are Yes,* and in Him Amen, to the glory of God through us." (2Co 1:20, emphasis added)

Unfortunately, it doesn't take much to break the connection of our spirit with His. God doesn't move away; we do. We are fragile in our spiritual life: we are shakable, unstable, doubting, fearful, condemnable, distractible, easily persuaded to unbelief. This is because we are being dominated by our natural man (carnal).

God's will is for us to work together (with Him), and we decide how much, when, what, where, and if. *It's amazing grace that comes to empower us, only as we believe.*

God will never over step what we really believe, what we really trust, what we really have faith for! God has subjected His Almighty power to our heart's believing in Him.

## A Good Illustration:

*Electricity* has been made available, but that doesn't mean we get to use it. We must be connected, and we must cooperate with the proper use of it. The power of electricity has been harnessed, and after we connect to it, we can use it. But who really decides *when* it will be manifested in our daily lives, the Electric Company or us? Who plugs in the lamp? Who turns on the appliance? We do.

*To the measure* we use it (faith in His grace), it will be measured back to us (Mark 4:24).

This is difficult to grasp, but the truth is: *"It isn't that God didn't."* God isn't holding back anything. If we think this way, it is because we don't believe He gave us all things in Christ. We don't believe that He's given us all things that pertain to life and godliness (2 Pet. 1:3). We don't believe He's already done it all. God is not the one who determines when. No—we are; now that's amazing.

## Another illustration:

A grandmother friend of ours loves to visit her granddaughters. She is at the ready when her daughter calls and says, "Mom, we'd love to have you come to see us." This grandmother is not deciding if she is going to come; she already wants to, and the only thing holding her back is her daughter's invitation. She doesn't want to intrude, push herself, or overstay her welcome into her daughter's life with her granddaughters. She would be there all the time, but she knows that would be overbearing; however, when she gets the call, she is already on her way. As far as the grandmother is concerned, the time is now! She is at the ready. She is waiting on her daughter's call.

Likewise, today (now) is the day of salvation! The Lord has helped us! We don't need to wait for His call! He is already calling to all of us, "Come unto Me and I will give you rest..." God has moved on our behalf, after nearly four thousand years, to bring us Christ. Today, He offers salvation, the power of His name, the gift of righteousness, and the complete forgiveness of our sins (past, present, and future). He has poured out His love, and the gift of His grace in His Spirit, and He is waiting on us to respond. He is waiting on us to believe Him, to acknowledge everything that is in us because of Christ, and to assert these provisions into our lives:

> "...that the sharing of *your faith may become effective by the acknowledgment of every good thing* which is in you in Christ Jesus." (Philemon 1:6, emphasis added)

## Conclusion: What a Strange Paradox!

God's already moved and decided. God's Spirit leads us and draws us to Himself; however, we determine when! God Almighty, who could force us, overwhelm us, and/or manipulate us, has decided that we decide.

> "*For as many as are led by the Spirit of God,* these are sons of God." (Ro 8:14, emphasis added)

**We are led to lead!** We are led to stop waiting on God to do something, when He's already done everything in Christ! Therefore, go in His name and do what Jesus would do. We don't wait upon the Lord anymore, because He's waiting on us to move in His grace by faith. Amen.

# CHAPTER IX

# DOES GOD ALLOW? OR ARE GOD'S HANDS TIED?

Here are several verses, with emphasis added, that represent the tension regarding God allowing, or not allowing things to happen:

> "No temptation has overtaken you except such as is common to man; but God is faithful, *who will not allow you to be tempted beyond* what you are able, but with the temptation will also make the way of escape, that you may be able to bear it." (1Co 10:13)

> *"He will not allow your foot to be moved*; He who keeps you will not slumber." (Ps 121:3)

And then verses like these:

> "In this manner, therefore, pray: Our Father in heaven, Hallowed be Your name. Your kingdom come. *Your will be done on earth as it is in heaven.*" (Matt. 6:9, 10)

> "Do not be deceived, God is not mocked; *for whatever a man sows, that he will also reap.* For he who sows to his flesh will of the flesh reap corruption, but he who sows to the Spirit will of the Spirit reap everlasting life." (Gal. 6: 7, 8)

*There Are Two Pillars of Opinion* in the Church that Confuse and Disarm Us: **God Allows, and God Chooses If And When He'll Intervene.** In this chapter, I want to address the first pillar.

## The First Pillar: Does God Allow?

Does God *allow* everything that happens in the earth? Does God *control* everything that goes on in the earth? The idea that God may not be involved with allowing things to happen often brings great fear into people's lives. The idea that God is not controlling everything that goes on also brings great fear. This tension is directly related to the sovereignty of God versus man's dominion (Chapter II). If God is not in control, who is? Does this mean things may happen to me that God can't stop?

The tension is also complicated by the fact that there are several levels of life that co-exist on the earth. The first level is the fallen state of man we are all born into. This level is natural, sin cursed, defiant of God's rule, and unable to grasp spiritual truths (I Cor. 2:14). This level is without God and hope in this world in any personal relationship (Eph. 2:12). The second level is the spiritual life and truths found in our born again position in Christ. These two different levels actually wrestle against each other:

> *"For the flesh lusts against the Spirit, and the Spirit against the flesh*; and these are contrary to one another, so that you do not do the things that you wish." (Ga 5:17, emphasis added)

It is vitally important that we affirm all scripture, but it is just as important that we have gotten the *update!* Jesus gave Paul, the apostle, the update on the new covenant, the new creation, removing the law's demands, and giving us the law of faith—the gospel of grace. We must remain in the place of His grace: armed, protected, and emboldened, able to overcome the deceptions and pitfalls of the evil ones. Now, let's consider how the first question

(Does God Allow?) can be answered by staying within the tension revealed in scripture.

Both of these questions reveal underlying opinions about God's activity and responsibility (God allows; why doesn't He intervene?) in this earth. Both of these opinions can have *negative effects* on our faith, depending upon our interpretations.

The first underlying opinion is: *God allows*. If we believe that God is *allowing* good things to happen to bad people, or bad things to happen to good people, *as in standing by watching and doing nothing*, we are going to frustrate ourselves and *cripple our faith* to trust God. The idea that *God is allowing* all that happens in life can be an indictment towards God's integrity, because *most* of what happens on the earth is **not** God's will.

The position of thinking that all things are under God's control *disarms us from resisting evil and standing up to threats* with a whole heart. This is because *we'll never know* if what is about to happen, or is happening, is from God, as *if He is allowing it to happen for some mysterious good.*

In truth, this confusion makes us passive, the result of this tension puts us in a place of doubt (we don't know). Furthermore, the apprehension of believing God is allowing things (anything) into our lives is crippling. We simply don't know what is from God and what isn't. In truth, we are remaining in the *wrong tension!*

God does work all things for good to those who love Him and are called according to His purpose (Rom. 8:28); however, that in itself, doesn't mean that God is *allowing or disallowing* anything into our lives. What it means is that whatever does happen, God will work for our good.

*This distinction is important* because believing that God is working all things for our good, as in allowing everything, places the good, bad, and *evil things, as if God is somehow determining them.*

The alternate position recognizes that God is working all things for our good in a kind of retroactive way. God *isn't allowing or disallowing* anything that happens: He's making all of it work for our good.

If God is controlling everything, then all the decisions people make would come under His responsibility; but that contradicts the testimony found in scripture. In fact, God cannot stop what *people* decide, and the consequences of those decisions, whether good, bad, or evil. The whole idea that God cannot stop something is just beyond the comprehension of some. How can God, who is almighty, be stopped? He can't be stopped by anyone, *but He has stopped Himself*! This is an important point of truth.

We must understand that at one level of human experience, the laws of sowing and reaping are automatic (Gal. 6:7). God is *not allowing or disallowing*, but the dominion He gave to man is in *full* effect (Duet. 30:19). If God intervenes, stopping the sowing and reaping process, He would be violating His own word (Num. 23:19). In the natural and fallen condition of humanity, God's laws are operating and governing our decision making and their consequences. The things that people do create a major part of the tension we experience in life. The reason the world is fallen, unfair, destructive, resulting in sickness, death, and evil, is because God's will is not being done here!

Many want to take *comfort in believing that God is orchestrating all the events in their lives.* Many want the comfort of believing that God is not going to *allow anything* into our lives that we cannot handle. After all, there are scriptures such as the one mentioned already (and repeated here):

> "No temptation has overtaken you except such as is common to man; but *God is faithful, who will not allow you to be tempted beyond what you are able,* but with the temptation will *also make the way of escape, that you may be able to bear it.*" (1Co 10:13, emphasis added)

However, is this verse speaking about God's sovereign power to control everything in our lives? What about the areas of life His sovereignty gave to us? Or, is this verse speaking to the Christian who is born again, and is walking according to the Spirit? This would include understanding that we are no longer under the dominion of the law (Rom. 6:4); we are to resist the curse of this world (Gal. 3:13); we submit to God and resist the devil (James 4:7).

Life is not simple. There are other players involved that affect our lives such as other people, demonic spirits, and the animal kingdom, along with God's will.

> "The thief does not come except to steal, and to kill, and to destroy. *I have come that they may have life, and that they may have it more abundantly.*" (John 10:10, emphasis added)

We are not to accept all the things that happen as if they are from God! Salvation in Christ changes everything, and puts us in a position to accept God's intervention (the Spirit's level); with God as our Father, we who were without hope now have great hope!

We moved from the kingdom of darkness, living in the world as *mere* men (I Cor. 3:3), to the kingdom of His beloved son (Col. 1:13). This too is huge. The first level is the kingdom of darkness under the curse; the second level is the kingdom of His beloved Son. We are born again, living in His grace by faith; operating in the authority of Jesus' name.

The tension created by affirming *both* opposing scriptural themes as true (God is sovereign but not in control of our decisions), *makes us dig deeper,* opens us up to revelation understanding, and keeps us closer to the straight and narrow truth.

In the kingdom of darkness, we were subject to all things before our salvation—because of the fall. We were vulnerable to the curse, sickness and disease, evil, and demonic oppression; but now, we are sons and daughters of Almighty God! Before, when we did not belong to God, we were not under His authority, nor under His umbrella of protection. Now however, we are *in* the gift of righteousness (Rom. 5:17), our prayers, which are according to His will, are effective and activate God's intervention.

The tension helps us to discern and activate the second level of spiritual life that is over and above the natural one. We see the dynamics of the old and new: the carnal nature and status, versus the new creation and authority. The old dominion position versus the new one!

In the new creation position, we submit to God and resist the devil (James 4:7). In this position, we take the name of Jesus and speak to the mountain to rebuke the curse (Mark 11:23, 24 & Gal. 3:13)! In this position, we cast away the law and live in newness of life (Rom. 7:6).

The world is fallen, and many decisions are being made by people that can and do affect our lives that God is *not allowing or disallowing*. There are weather catastrophes such as: earthquakes, tornadoes, and storms that rage. God is *not allowing or disallowing them*. They happen because of the fall from God's grace, when man lost control of nature (in particular, the changed world after the flood of Noah, 2 Pet. 2:5).

If we believe that God is permitting these things, we will not exercise our position of righteousness in Christ and rebuke them from affecting us, or others (Jesus rebuked the winds and the waves, Mat. 8:26). In Christ, God has brought us *grace and truth* to restore our dominion over sin and its consequences (Rom. 6:14); this is giving back to us what Adam and Eve lost.

We are the ones in the driver's seat (Eph. 1: 30 & 1:20)! We now have the right to accept or not accept the things that come our way. For instance, when doctors or reporters tell us it is *flu season*, is God *allowing* the flu? The flu itself is a product of the curse of the law (Deut. 28), and since we have been redeemed from the curse in Christ's atonement, we need to realize our authority to resist this curse (Gal. 3:13). We must take a stand and deny the flu any right to come upon us, knowing that God, through the blood of Christ, already gave us provision over it in the new birth.

We find therefore, *great comfort* in God when we realize what Christ did on the cross on our behalf. We find *great comfort* in realizing that God has provided all things that pertain to life and godliness in our salvation experience (2 Pet. 1:1-3). We find *great comfort* in knowing God, knowing peace, and *discerning this matter* to rebuke evil, the curse, and fallen weather patterns.

Greater is God in us than he that is in the world (I John 4:4). Our comfort is found in being born again, standing in righteousness, letting the peace of God rule and *taking the authority of the name of Jesus to command God's will be done in our life!*

This is a basic truth that cannot be violated: *God cannot save one single soul until that soul prays in Jesus' name.* If we understand this, then understand the importance of prayer, for ourselves and others, by declaring in His name! There are things that God has put into our realm of control through the New Covenant. When He gave us authority and dominion in Christ, He makes it subject to us. *This means His hands are tied to ours.* If we don't act upon His name and provision in Jesus, He can't do it for us.

## God's Sovereignty Provided Choice in Dominion

As long as we believe that God's Sovereignty means that He controls everything, and therefore, is responsible for all that happens in life, we will remain in a position of weakness and confusion (our doubts makes us passive—the wrong tension). This takes away dominion and choice as if it has no meaning— *removing the right tension!*

Although we may be exercising faith to believe that God's sovereignty means that everything that comes into our life is under His control, we are being misled. We have removed the tension of God giving us authority and power through Christ on earth!

> "Behold, *I give you the authority* to trample on serpents and scorpions, and over all the power of the enemy,

and nothing shall by any means hurt you." (Lu 10:19, emphasis added)

We believe God is sovereign and almighty, the creator of all that exists. This doesn't mean that God is controlling all that happens upon the earth. If heaven is God's throne, and His will is done perfectly there, then Jesus teaching us to pray God's "will be done on earth as it is heaven," has meaning (Luke 11:2). It has meaning if the earth is fallen, cursed, and His will is not being done here.

## God Allowed It!

Someone might argue that sin and the fall could only happen if God allowed it. This is true. God could have set up the situation where no sin and no fall could occur—which means no actual dominion of man genuinely exists. When God gave Adam and Eve dominion and choice, it could only be real if there were choices other than God's will.

By giving opportunity for decisions to be made, other than God's will, does that make God responsible for our choices? No. What it does allow is freedom to decide, but it does not mean God *wants* those choices to be made. What it does mean is that God's *gift of dominion* provides for choices that are against His will.

If God is sovereign and almighty, how is it possible to stop God's will? It is stopped every time God's will is not being chosen—when our choices are not His choices. He would be violating His own word to stop our dominion, and God cannot lie (Heb. 6:19).

Simply then, whose choices are made constantly upon the earth? The answer is obvious that man's choices dominate, not God's. If man's choices are responsible for evil, does that mean God is allowing it? Certainly not! God's command was for us to exercise our dominion in agreement with His Will. When we choose to take the *gift of dominion* and use it for evil, God cannot stop it, or He'd be lying about having given us dominion in the first place:

> "Then God said, "Let Us make man in Our image, according to Our likeness; *let them have dominion* over the fish of the sea, over the birds of the air, and over the cattle, *over all the earth* and over every creeping thing that creeps on the earth." (Ge 1:26, emphasis added)

> "I call heaven and earth as witnesses today against you, *that I have set before you life and death,* blessing and cursing; *therefore choose life that* both you and your descendants may live..." (De 30:19, emphasis added)

God set before us life and death, blessing and cursing; but then said, "Choose life that both you and your descendants may live." If we decide to do things our way, we are choosing for ourselves death and the curse. God isn't allowing it, as in standing by watching, as if He could stop it at any time, but doesn't. Once He gave dominion to man, it was out of His hands and into ours.

The tension is that God's sovereignty is actually being realized *through our choices.* We remove the tension from scripture if we say our choices show that God is *not sovereign,* because it is His dominion we are using to make them (Video Game Analogy).


## Example:

If a parent gives an adult son a car (with ownership), and that son decides to use that car in ways the parent would not choose, there is nothing the parent can do. If the parent tries to take back ownership of the car, the son could take the matter to court and the law would back him up. Furthermore, the parent would be violating his/her own word to do this.

The gift of ownership means, "I have dominion." This illustration speaks to the relationship of dominion in a way that most of us can understand. Would the parent be responsible for the son's choices? Would the parent be "allowing" the son to do wrong things with the car? Certainly not; however, did the parent allow for it *as a potential*?

In other words, did the parent's choice to give the gift of ownership to the son provide, or allow for evil? The answer is yes, and this is where there is truth in the sentiments, "God is allowing."

We must discern however, that providing *for a potential evil* doesn't mean we are allowing that evil to continue, once dominion is bestowed. We come to understand this distinction, only by keeping the tension between acknowledging God's sovereignty and the gift of dominion to humanity.

In providing choice, ownership, and dominion, there is the possibility of using it in evil ways; however, once ownership is given, even though it is providing for choices other than God's own, *the responsibility passes onto the owner.*

On the one side, God is allowing evil (or wrong choices) *as a potential,* if He is giving true dominion and freedom to decide. But once dominion is given, God is no longer responsible, as in allowing, wrong choices and evil to continue to prevail. He didn't want the wrong choices in the first place, *but it was the consequence of giving dominion* that wrong choices are made.

Once the dominion was bestowed upon man, God was no longer in a position to *allow or disallow* wrong choices. One could argue that God allowed the possibility of evil *at the beginning,* but one cannot argue, in truth, that God is *allowing or disallowing* evil to continue—*it is in man's dominion.*

## The Video Game Analogy Revisited:

Think of a video game again, where the programmer has programmed all of the options and consequences of every decision. The creator has also placed in life, all of the options and consequences of every decision, even providing for evil to be committed. Evil is using things in a way God would not use them. Evil is perverting the original purpose of something for selfish gains and purposes. A simple example would be the creation of a pencil, which has a wonderful use in writing; however, if we use that pencil for stabbing someone's eye out, then that would be an evil use of something created for good.

God's sovereignty is programmed into life just like a video game has been programmed by its creator. The laws that govern life are: everything reproduces after its own kind (Gen. 6:20), and we reap what we sow (Gal. 6:7). It means everything has a consequence, or a cause and effect.

When we play a video game, we enter that game world through a controller. We take on the life of a player and begin to make decisions. The more advanced the game, the more options are provided, but as we all know, every *decision's consequence in the game is predetermined*. The program has already planned out every move and what will happen; yet, we play the game because our decisions along the path are varied, giving us *programmed choice*.

God's sovereignty in life is the same. His judgments are in the earth (Ps. 105:7). The laws that govern are here, and our every decision has consequences within the game of life. We still have choices, because God has set before us good and evil, blessing and cursing, giving us dominion within the predetermined programs of life. There is nothing outside of the programming that can happen in a video game; likewise, there is nothing outside of God's sovereignty and created order that can happen in life.

**Special Aside**: the demons' only true power over anyone is the *law of God* (I Cor. 15:56). They are deceiving each one of us to make decisions that will bring the curse back upon us. They can possess someone who continues to proceed towards evil, seeking to find spirits, and yielding by giving them permission to control him/her. Once possession takes place, it is as if the demon is playing the game of life through an individual (There are biblical examples of minimal powers expressed through possessed people in scripture).

When someone argues that God is allowing evil to happen and bad things to come our way, this ignores or forgets that once the game of life is engaged, the programming (law) takes over.

God allowed for it in the programming, as far as dominion is concerned, but He is not responsible for the consequences of our decisions in life. He cannot *allow nor disallow* once dominion has been given, speaking from a purely natural perspective (describing the kingdom of darkness), and all things being under the law.

The tension is found in asking the question: "How can these apparently contradicting principles both be true?" When we affirm both, it keeps us in a place where the depth of life becomes understandable. We get wisdom that leads us and keeps us closer to who God really is, and how He set things up in the earth.

## The Game Changer!

God has not left us to our demise of falling under the curse of the law, and being oppressed by the demonic in this life. **He has helped us** (2 Cor. 2:6), and sent His only begotten Son to deliver us from our sin. He provided for the Holy Spirit to redeem us and make us born again (John 3:16). God does not want us to receive the consequences of our decisions, especially in regards to sinful choices.

*The born again experience changes everything.* We, who were once under the law, now reign in Christ, through grace *over* the law (Rom. 5:17). We, who were held by the law, now have dominion in grace *over* sin (Rom. 7:6). We who suffered the curse, now rule and reign through God's Word, through the Holy Spirit, and through faith, as we awaken to righteousness (I Cor. 15:34)!

We now go from being mere men and constantly defeated, to victory in Christ Jesus having the same ministry, work, power, and authority in His name (John 14:12)! We go from being in bondage to sin nature, to being God's Sons and Daughters! We are His ambassadors, and His ministers of reconciliation, having been given the *Word of reconciliation* (2 Cor. 5:18). We are the bride of Christ; we are His workmanship; we are the redeemed, and *we are the beloved* (Eph. 2:10)*!* We were outcasts bound in trespasses and sins, but now we are accepted, forgiven, and given *the gift of righteousness.*

> "For if by the one man's offense death reigned through the one, much more those who receive abundance of grace and of the *gift of righteousness* will *reign in life* through the One, Jesus Christ..." (Ro 5:17, emphasis added)

We were once defeated and without hope, held in bondage to the law: for every sin we sowed, we (collectively) reaped in true justice. However, now we are made righteous through the blood of the Savior. He took our sin upon himself and gave us *His righteousness,* so that we can now overcome what once held us (Col. 2:13, 14).

# CHAPTER X

# IS GOD RESPONSIBLE FOR EVERYTHING OR NOT? WHY DOESN'T GOD INTERVENE?

In this chapter, I want to address the second pillar (opinion) that causes confusion in the church.

## The Second Pillar: Does "God Choose if and When He'll Intervene?"

The second pillar (or opinion) is just as bad in leaving us defenseless and confused; but it does logically follow that if God allowed certain things to happen in our lives, why didn't He intervene? If we believe that God is allowing the things that happen in life, and many of those things are bad, then we are naturally going to ask why? Why did He allow them? If He had the right to stop bad things, why didn't He?

The answers to these questions, however Biblical they may appear, are going to be wrong, *if the questions themselves are wrong.* We will not get a right answer to a wrong question. It may appear to be answered and it may appear to be right, but the truth is, we are wrangling over things that are in a real sense *"out of bounds."*

Are these issues legitimate from a Biblical perspective? There will be arguments and scriptures to support the ideas that God allows and God chooses if He'll intervene (especially from the book of Job); however, if we stay true to God's *dominion gift to man* (stay in the tension), we should at least acknowledge the possibility that God allowing is out of bounds!

Furthermore, if we understand that God is not in a position *to allow or disallow,* having given dominion to man, *then His arbitrary intervention would also be out of bounds!* This speaks to a fundamental level of life's existence, or game rules, with man in charge in the *kingdom of darkness.*

## Why Doesn't God Intervene?

This question misses the *greatest gift* of all: Jesus Christ. If we believe that Jesus is the Son of God incarnated into human flesh, then there is no greater intervention possible! The question misses the mark because *it is not recognizing how God has intervened!*

> *"For God so loved the world* that He gave His only begotten Son, that whoever believes in Him should not perish but have everlasting life." (Joh 3:16, emphasis added)

What more could God do to intervene than send His only begotten Son? What greater cost, or mission could exist, than God coming Himself to save us? Has God intervened? *Absolutely He has and to the greatest extent!*

God intervened in lesser ways prior to His incarnation. We see that in the Old Testament with the patriarchs, the prophets, and the law with its blessings and curses, and Moses the deliverer. We can also see that *none of these* lesser attempts to intervene could possibly save and make us born again. For example, the law could make no one perfect (Heb. 7:19). What Jesus has done is redeem us to the uttermost; *it is a complete intervention!*

> "Therefore He is also able to *save to the uttermost* those who come to God through Him, since He always lives

to make intercession for them." (Heb 7:25, emphasis added)

The scriptures testify that no man can be justified and made right with God through keeping the law. *The law is powerless to change hearts and cleanse us from sin* (Heb. 10:1). The law, as holy as it is, only has one purpose: to expose our sins and condemn us in unrighteousness (Gal. 3:19). The law shows us that we fall short of God's glory, and that we do not have the love of God in us. It is as if we have all been trying to play the video game of life and no one can beat it. We all die, we are failing, and we all are subject and vulnerable to the game's curses.

*God's intervention is the Messiah,* who comes as one of us, lives as one of us, and beats the law of life for us. Jesus beat the game by living sinless, and then offering Himself as a sacrifice for the sins of the whole world. He offered Himself as the one righteous man to take the sins of the unrighteous, to satisfy the law's judgments against us (Col. 2:13, 14). One man Adam caused the curse to come to all; one man Jesus provided the way of escape and salvation to all (Rom. 5:18).

It is God who is satisfied in the sacrifice of Christ. It is God who is finding peace within Himself concerning our rebellion, actions, and willful misconduct (Chapter IV). It is God who is bringing peace between Himself, as Holy and just, with sinful man. God satisfies Himself in fulfilling the law's requirements against us, that every action and decision we made has a consequence. Jesus said this:

> "Do not think that *I came* to destroy the Law or the Prophets. I did not come to destroy *but to fulfill.*" (Mt 5:17, emphasis added)

**Special Note**: Once Jesus beat the law's requirements against us, it was like He beat the "game of life." When anyone beats a video game at every level, and the challenge is over, there are some games that provide "cheat codes." Cheat codes allow the victorious player to change the game, jump levels, overcome obstacles, and in a sense dominate as if they were a type of god. They would have powers beyond someone who hasn't beaten it. Jesus rose from the dead and gave us His name, His peace, His faith, His Spirit, and His commission; all of which through God's grace, make us dominate and override the world's kingdom of darkness. This works in our life according to the power of Christ in us—as we believe it (Eph. 3:20). Amen.

Jesus came to fulfill the law's justice against sinners, and He did it. He intervened on our behalf. Once an obligation is fulfilled, it is no longer enforced. Once a debt is paid, it is no longer owed.

> "But *God demonstrates His own love toward us*, in that while we were still sinners, Christ died for us." (Ro 5:8, emphasis added)

His intercession is huge! Not only does He save us from our sins, but He makes us one with Him and the Father. He takes us from under all things, *to above all things* in Christ Jesus. As we look at the life of Jesus and how He lived, the works that He did, the things He preached, the love He demonstrated, *we are seeing what He made us!*

*Jesus came to re-produce Himself as a seed re-produces itself with thousands!*

His mission was to restore what was lost in the fall; that we would take on His commission to do what He did (Matt. 28:20). That we would have the same attitude towards life as He did!

> "Most assuredly, I say to you, unless a grain of wheat falls into the ground *and dies, it remains alone*; but if it dies, *it produces much grain*." (Joh 12:24, emphasis added)

> "For whom He foreknew, He also predestined *to be* conformed to the image of His Son, that He might be

the *firstborn among many brethren.*" (Ro 8:29, emphasis added)

We have been given the same Spirit, with the same authority, as if we were Christ walking in the earth again, to do the same things He did.

> "Most assuredly, I say to you, he who believes in Me, the *works that I do he will do also; and greater works* than these he will do, because I go to My Father." (Joh 14:12, emphasis added)

One could have argued that God wanted the world to know that Jesus is the Messiah, therefore, God commissioned Him to heal, to deliver, and to set free to show He is Lord. Certainly, that is true; yet, *Jesus' mission and then re-commission* of His disciples was to do the very works He did!

The Great Commission has often in our day been presented to mean salvation in the new birth; what has not been presented is how much that commission included healing, deliverance, and setting the captives free! In other words, the Great Commission is *"Two-Fold."* The first part is meant to help us accomplish the second part. Listen to Jesus' commissioning of the twelve apostles and then the seventy. He sent them out two by two. They were to heal the sick and then preach the kingdom of God is near:

> *"Heal the sick, cleanse the lepers, raise the dead, cast out demons.* Freely you have received, freely give." (Mt. 10:8, emphasis added)

> "He sent them *to preach the kingdom of God and to heal the sick.*" (Luke 9:2, emphasis added)

> *"And heal the sick there,* and say to them, 'The kingdom of God has come near to you.'" (Luke 10:9, emphasis added)

The laborers were meant to show God's power to forgive, deliver, and then preach the kingdom of God! The same is just as true today as it was then and even more so since Jesus has been glorified, and the Holy Spirit sent into the hearts of believers!

> "Then He said to His disciples, 'The harvest truly *is* plentiful, but the *laborers are few.*
> *Therefore pray the Lord of the harvest to send out laborers* into His harvest." (Mt 9:37, 38, emphasis added)

We have the same Spirit that raised Christ from the dead dwelling in us, to do the same things for the same reasons!

> "But if the Spirit of Him who raised Jesus from the dead *dwells in you,* He who raised Christ from the dead *will also give life to your mortal bodies through His Spirit who dwells in you.*" (Ro 8:11, emphasis added)

This is also considered the **Great Commission!**

> "Go therefore and make disciples of all the nations, baptizing them in the name of the Father and of the Son and of the Holy Spirit, *teaching them to observe all things that I have commanded you;* and lo, I am with you always, *even* to the end of the age." (Matt. 28:19, 20, emphasis added)

Somehow this verse (20) gets forgotten, or left out; however, Jesus commanded the apostles to make disciples, *"teaching them to observe all things that Jesus commanded them!"* That includes preaching the gospel and healing the sick, as I have written.

God's will is to manifest His glory through His sons and daughters in the name of Jesus! The name of Jesus is Lord, deliverer, redeemer, savior, healer, protector, provider, and all wisdom and power! We are to go in His name to do what Jesus did! We are commissioned to be His ambassadors and ministers of reconciliation! These verses speak to this, emphasis added:

> "*Now then, we are ambassadors for Christ,* as though God were pleading through us: we implore *you* on Christ's behalf, be reconciled to God." (2Co 5:20)

> "Now all things *are* of God, who has reconciled us to Himself through Jesus Christ, *and has given us the ministry of reconciliation...*" (2Co 5:18)

> "And whatever you ask *in My name,* that I will do, *that the Father may be glorified in the Son.*" (Joh 14:13)

> "*By this My Father is glorified, that you bear much fruit;* so you will be My disciples." (Joh 15:8)

Consider these "Just as" statements that Jesus makes towards all believers, with emphasis added:

> "*As You* sent Me into the world, I also have sent them into the world." (Joh 17:18)

> "...that they all may be one, **as** You, Father, *are* in Me, and I in You; *that they also may be one in Us,* that the world may believe that You sent Me.
> *And the glory which You gave Me I have given them,* that they may be one *just as* We are one: I in them, and You in Me; that they may be made perfect in one, and that the world may know that You have sent Me, *and have loved them as You have loved Me.*" (Joh 17:21-23)

> "So Jesus said to them again, 'Peace to you! *As the Father has sent Me, I also send you.*'" (Joh 20:21)

## Conclusion:

I could write pages and pages to verify God's intention to make us *"just as,"* and *"just like,"* His Son in this life. God's intervention wasn't just to call off the dogs, pick us up and clean off the dirt, to fix our wounds, and set us on our feet to go off and do it all over again. No, His intervention was to create for Himself sons and daughters who will rule and reign in life through Jesus' name (Rom. 5:17). We have an astounding power and authority over life itself now, through faith in His grace. This power works through His love in us (Gal. 5:6).

God's grace has restored us to dominion over sin and over the curse of the law, to exercise His will upon the earth. The following verses speak to this, with emphasis added:

> "For if by the one man's offense death reigned through the one, much more those who receive abundance of grace and of the *gift of righteousness will reign in life through the One, Jesus Christ...*" (Ro 5:17)

> "Love has been perfected among us in this: that we may have boldness in the day of judgment; because as He is, *so are we in this world.*" (1Jo 4:17)

Our prayers and our declarations, in His name and through His Word, activate the Spirit to bring about God's will in our life: to provide, to protect, to guide, to save, to heal, to restore, to deliver, and to have His presence never leave us nor forsake us.

As we submit to God's life, we resist the devil and he flees from us. As we come under God's authority, we exercise His authority: As Jesus spoke to the fig tree and cursed it for not producing figs, and it withered and died; as He spoke to the winds and waves, "peace be still" and they obeyed Him; as He spoke to cast out demons and they left; as He spoke to sickness and disease, healing all who came to Him; *likewise, God has given us this same ministry of reconciliation and intervention!*

We are God's body: His hands, feet, mouth, eyes, ears, and army upon the earth to bring about life, and it more abundantly (John 10:10). As strange as this might sound, just as we cannot do anything without our body on the earth, likewise, God cannot *allow or disallow* anything on the earth without His body—we are His body!

## Why Doesn't God Intervene?

He has, in the greatest possible way, and then turned that intervention over to His body on the earth. The reason we ask this question is because we have not understood dominion and *how God did intervene!*

He says to us, "go in my name" and do the things I would do. Heal the sick, raise the dead, cast out the demons, cleanse the lepers; freely you have received, freely give.

Why doesn't God intervene? When we realize exactly how much God *has* intervened, the whole question becomes embarrassing. God has helped us; He has intervened beyond our ability to measure:

> "For He says: 'In an acceptable time *I have heard you,* And *in the day of salvation **I have helped you.**"* Behold, now *is* the accepted time; behold, now *is* the day of salvation." (2Co 6:2, emphasis added)

## An Important Final Thought!

One final thought concerning the issue, "God chooses when and if He'll intervene." As was the case with "God allows," *this presupposes that God has the freedom to act or not act, to stop or not stop, in the kingdom of darkness.* This is not true.

We must understand that God's *hands were tied,* according to His own promise, when He gave us dominion. Now, because of the new creation, God can act through His body, the body of Christ, the true believers in this world; however, *that intervention is subject to us!*

We continually fall back into the misconception that God is acting sovereignly, *without restraints,* in dealing with man upon the earth—*not so.* He has subjected His intervention to the Name of Jesus and through His body, the born again believers. It is not that we are waiting on God to intervene at any time; it is God waiting on us to act in His name to intervene at any time (Chapter VIII).

God hasn't abolished man's dominion, but has provided the way, the truth, and the life (John 14:6) to restore **righteous dominion** upon the earth in man through Jesus Christ! Amen. In other words, *God has tied His hands to ours.*

This leads to another misconception that God is waiting to act, or to intervene, *in some future moment.* God has already acted and decided when He sent Jesus to redeem us. God has already poured out His blessing and His love through the Holy Spirit (Rom. 5:5). God has already authorized us to go in Jesus' name to make disciples, to deliver, to heal the sick, to cast out demons, and to cleanse the lepers.

It is in understanding that grace has already done it, and finished the work (God intervened) in the atonement, that we grasp how God has set things up. We got here by remaining in the tension that God is not allowing anything, and that He has intervened in the most amazing way. *God is now waiting on us to get it and to act upon what He's done*—that is faith in action in His grace.

# CHAPTER XI

# TO JUDGE OR NOT TO JUDGE!

If there is a particular tension that is experienced more than this one, I don't know what it is. Compare these two verses as an example of the tension over this question, "Do we judge or don't we?"

Jesus said:

> *"Judge not, and you shall not be judged.* Condemn not, and you shall not be condemned. Forgive, and you will be forgiven." (Lu 6:37, emphasis added)

Then Paul wrote:

> "But he who is spiritual *judges all things,* yet he himself is *rightly* judged by no one." (1Co 2:15, emphasis added)

When Jesus spoke these words, it was to people who were under the law. No one could keep the law, and in truth, no one can stop judging. This was like saying to all of us, "Stop breathing!" We can no more stop judging than we can stop breathing, eating, talking, or thinking. We were made to judge! We were made to make decisions (judgments) about life. We cannot exercise dominion without making judgments. We cannot exercise choice without judgments; therefore, there isn't a day, an hour, or even minutes passing by, when we are not making them.

When Jesus said this, it was like saying to all of us, "You are in trouble!" Since we cannot stop judging, then we are all under judgment. This truth alone makes this tension universal. We are all under the judgment of the law for judging *the way we do.*

Having said that, what then are we supposed to do? When it comes to judging there is more to consider. Let me present to you this truth: "It's not whether we judge; it is which judgment is the best judgment to judge with!" The tension concerning judgment involves *judging according to the flesh or judging according to the Spirit.*

## Under the Law We Were Responsible to Judge

Under the law, we were responsible to make things right, to correct, to bring to account, and to hold up the standard, so that good won over evil. Under the law, we were to make judgments to keep it, so that we could be blessed and our children after us:

> "I call heaven and earth as witnesses today against you, that I have set before you life and death, blessing and cursing; *therefore, choose life that both you and your descendants may live."* (De 30:19, emphasis added)

When self-centered people make judgments (decisions), they are not going to be along the lines of God's love. Most, if not all, of the world's suffering comes from people making judgments according to sin nature. *This causes tension between us!*

If we resist our natural tendency to judge according to the flesh, and judge according to the Spirit, we stay in tension against our own nature (putting it down), but remain at peace with God (and most of the time with each other). Many of us have heard this statement: "Judge the sin; not the sinner." This begins to expose *the tension* involving our propensity towards judging as a by-product of our sin nature.

The tension involves judging people according to the law, our standards, and even the standards of others. We hold others to account, judging their motives, while often only judging our own actions. We all know about double standards, and readily call out anyone when practicing them.

We all know what it feels like to be judged and condemned, not only by others, but from within our own hearts. The law itself is perfectly, constantly, and penetratingly, judging every one of us, twenty-four hours a day and seven days a week (the natural man). The law is relentless in bringing all of us under condemnation for our sins. The tension within each of us about our own guilt and condemnation is common to humanity (sin and guilt consciousness). The tension can be so great that some break down, become mentally unstable, retreat or escape reality, in order to find some kind of relief.

## Under Grace This Changed

We are to follow in Christ's steps, who did not live life for Himself (Phil. 2:5-8) but yielded to the Spirit completely. When others reviled (Judged) Him, He did not revile back; when He suffered threats, lies, manipulations, He wasn't threatened, but stayed in peace. Jesus committed Himself to the One who judges righteously (I Pet. 2:23). *Jesus showed us how we are to judge according to the Spirit!*

## Jesus Lived to the One Who Judges Righteously

One of the reasons we are fretful, fearful, anxious, and *have lost peace*, is because we are judging twenty-four seven according to the flesh. We judge this person or that one, this situation or that, read between the lines, jump to conclusions, accuse in our thoughts and words, run down our neighbor, and get *entangled* with this plot or that vain speculation (much to do with fear). Jesus didn't do this and said to us:

> "For with what judgment you judge, *you will be judged; and with the measure you use, it will be measured back to you.*" (Mt 7:2, emphasis added)

With every effort we make to judge, we are bringing back judgment upon ourselves. We, in essence, have fallen from grace and walked back under the law. The law, with no partiality and without passion, brings back the same measure we put in.

How do we know we are back under the law? Check within our hearts. *Have we lost our peace?* Are we angry, frustrated, resentful, and even bitter? Consider the opening phrase of this verse: "For with what judgment you judge..." It matters greatly which judgment we employ in our lives. Do we judge according to the flesh, or according to the Spirit?

## Let's Look At What Jesus Did!

> Joh 8:15 "You *judge* according to the flesh; I *judge* no one."

Jesus said that natural man judges according to the flesh. This begins to make the distinction between judging according to the flesh and judging according to the Spirit. Jesus, who walked in full grace and anointing in the Spirit said, "I judge no one."

That seems impossible to the natural man. Jesus couldn't possibly be like us; He must have been God in the flesh, for only God has the power to not judge. Yet, the gospel of Jesus' incarnation revealed that He was fully human (although being fully God), and while living upon the earth lived just as a human being (Phil. 2:5-8).

Then Jesus went on to say:

> "*And yet if I do judge,* My judgment is true; for I am not alone, but I *am* with the Father who sent Me." (Joh 8:16, emphasis added)

Jesus judges no one; but He said, *"And yet if I do judge, My judgment is true."* What does this mean? Does Jesus judge or not?

Let me put it this way: when people tell us that this person or that person is biased (implying that people can be unbiased), they are saying that person's comments are not valid.

The truth of the matter is this: *no one is unbiased.* We are all influenced by perspectives, experiences, our natural mind, and sin nature. The answer in life *isn't to find truth in the unbiased,* but to realize it is about *which bias is the best bias to be biased with.*

Jesus is saying He does not judge according to the flesh! However, if He did judge (while in the flesh as a human being), *His judgment is true,* because it is not His judgment, it is the Father's judgment. As I was stating: "It isn't about not judging at all, but which is the best judgment to be judging with!"

*When we judge according to the flesh,* our judgment is going to be wrong, we are going to be blinded, misguided, presumptuous and more. We need to judge according to the Spirit. When God chose David to be king, for example, all of his brothers were older, bigger, stronger, maybe even better looking, but what did the scripture testify? Samuel the prophet was examining each of David's brothers to see if any of them were God's choice as king:

> "But the LORD said to Samuel, "Do not look at his appearance or at the height of his stature, because I have refused him. *For the LORD does not see as man sees; for man looks at the outward appearance, but the LORD looks at the heart."* (1Sa 16:7, emphasis added)

Then God told Samuel to anoint David king of Israel. The flesh judges outwardly, jumping to conclusions, blinded by pride and prestige, money, favoritism, selfishness, greed, lusts, and surely we can all understand, without full knowledge. When we judge according to the flesh, we are removing the tension involved with judging according to the Spirit—we simply ignore it.

When Jesus judged, He did it as a man under spiritual authority and guidance. His judgments, in truth, were not even His own. Consider these verses about Jesus' testimony concerning judgments, with emphasis added:

> "I have many things to say and to *judge* concerning you, but He who sent Me is true; *and I speak to the world those things which I heard from Him.*" (Joh 8:26)

> "And if anyone hears My words *and does not believe, I do not judge him*; for I did not come to *judge the world but to save the world.*
> He who rejects Me, and does not receive My words, *has that which judges him--the word that I have spoken will judge him in the last day.*" (Joh 12:47, 48)

Jesus is saying that as a man, I don't involve myself with judging according to the flesh—at all! Further, He wasn't sent to judge the world, but to save it. If He judged, He judged according to the Spirit; even when He judged, it was not Him, but the words that He spoke, that judged. The words that Jesus spoke are not His words, but the things which He heard from the Father to speak.

## Judging, but Not Their Own

When someone is under authority and has been given the task of making judgments or decisions, they are not making those judgments *on their own*. When a subordinate is ordered by a superior to command, to pass on instructions, and inform others of a decision, that authority is not their own! This is exactly what Jesus is saying in this verse:

> "I can of Myself do nothing. *As I hear, I judge; and My judgment is righteous,* because *I do not seek My own will but the will of the Father who sent Me.*" (Joh 5:30, emphasis added)

When Jesus says, "Judge not..." He is saying stop acting like *mere* men do. Stop looking at life as a natural man. Stop fussing, stop fuming, stop fretting, and stop worrying, as if it was all on us—according to the flesh. *It stopped being on us when we gave ourselves to the Lord and became born again.* How do we know this? It is because Jesus judged according the Spirit, under the authority of the Father, and the word tells us to judge in the same way!

## Let Peace Rule All Judgment

We are to live in the Spirit, *in newness of life,* and let the peace of God rule our hearts. When we judge according to the flesh, we are acting on our own—losing our peace. We are judging from our perspective, our knowledge, and our bias.

When Jesus said:

> *"Peace I leave with you, My peace I give to you;* not as the world gives do I give to you. *Let not your heart be troubled, neither let it be afraid."* (Joh 14:27, emphasis added)

He was telling us to stop living like the world does and live as He did—in the Father's peace. God, the Father, judges righteously, He knows what has happened, what was behind it, and what motivated it. He knows all things; what do we really know?

> "Beloved**,** *do not avenge yourselves,* but *rather* give place to wrath; for it is written, *'Vengeance is Mine,* I will repay,' says the Lord." (Ro 12:19, emphasis added)

We are admonished again and again *to put on the new man* in righteousness and holiness, walking according to the Spirit, so that we do not fulfill the lusts of the flesh (Gal. 5:16). We are cursing ourselves when we operate in the flesh to judge, evaluate, and bring others to account, because with what measure we put out, it comes back to us. The place of peace is under authority submitting to God's rule and reign in our lives, which means to stop judging *according to the flesh.*

> "And let *the peace of God rule in your hearts, to which also you were called* in one body; and be thankful." (Col 3:15, emphasis added)

## The Right Question

Therefore, the question becomes: *which is the best judgment we are to judge with!* We are to walk according to the Spirit, and by the Spirit, judge all things.

> "But he who is spiritual *judges all things,* yet he himself is *rightly* judged by no one." (1Co 2:15, emphasis added)

When *we* judge, it is of the flesh; when we allow the Spirit to judge through us, we judge all things righteously, because it is received from the Lord. As one under authority, our judgment is not even our own, and in this place we are guarding our peace and staying in it. Let us stay submitted to God, and resist the devil by not taking the bait to get us to judge according to the flesh.

## Guard Our Peace!

Walk in peace, stay in peace, and guard our peace, because that is the place of power in the Spirit. When we lose our peace, we *lose our place in Christ and step out from under grace and authority.* This is what the enemy wants us to do.

Meditate on spiritual things, and do not let your heart be troubled by the cares of this world. Do not take the bait of defending your life and becoming entangled with judgments, evaluations, and accountabilities. This only leads us *to lose our peace* and become in bondage to the law again (Gal. 5:1).

Peace is power! When we remain in His peace, His power is released to work in our lives. When we are in peace, we are not striving (tension) against the Spirit; however, from the natural (man) side of things, we'll experience tension because the flesh lusts against the Spirit.

In His peace, we see things we'd never see. In His Peace, we say things that we'd never say. In His peace, we know things we'd never know. In peace, we know, see, and speak, as if the very oracles of God. We get to use His words, His eyes, and His knowing. His stuff works far better!

We are not out on our own, we are under His authority, and that brings peace and power to every situation. This is the meaning of the following verse:

> "If anyone speaks, *let him speak* as the *oracles of God.* If anyone ministers, *let him do it as with the ability which God supplies, that in all things God may be glorified* through Jesus Christ, to whom belong the glory and the dominion forever and ever. Amen." (1Pe 4:11, emphasis added)

God's grace supplies the answers (judgments), the responses, the actions we are to take, as if God was calling every play of our life—and that is His will. As we have come to understand, *the law* demands and places the responsibility upon us. We are to set things right, we are to judge rightly; however, *under grace* God supplies. God gives the words, the answers, the righteous judgments we are to live by.

He corrects, He sets things straight on our behalf as we stay in His peace! Remember, Jesus is the Prince of Peace and in that peace God's kingdom is manifest—His will is done.

## We Don't Even Judge Ourselves!

The apostle Paul wrote:

> "But with me it is a very small thing that I should be judged by you or by a human court. In fact, *I do not even judge myself.*" (1Co 4:3, emphasis added)

Most people are harder on themselves than others would ever be. That is because we know what we've done, what we think, what we've said, *and it ain't pretty*. Many of us are readily convicted of guilt and have areas that we'd never want others to see or know. We don't need anyone else to judge us, since we already do a good enough job on our own.

Then when it comes to the law and knowing that God is going to hold us accountable for every idle word we have ever spoken—let alone the thoughts of our heart—well, there is no hope.

What in the world is Paul talking about when he dismisses the judgment of others and then says he doesn't even judge himself? This is crazy. Good for you, Brother Paul that you don't judge yourself. God must have put on you a special anointing that is beyond most of us.

## The Answer from God's Word

When I belonged to me, I was responsible; when I was bought by Christ that makes Him responsible. When I belonged to me, I was the judge; now that I belong to Him, He is the judge.

If all my sin is forgiven because He paid the debt I could not pay, then there is no more to be paid. My forgiveness means I've been given righteousness through His blood. If the judge of all the earth says I'm not guilty, who am I to say I am?

Listen again to this passage from Romans 8:32-39, emphasis added:

"He who did not spare His own Son, but delivered Him up for us all, *how shall He not with Him also freely give us all things?*

*Who shall bring a charge against God's elect? It is God who justifies.*

*Who is he who condemns? It is Christ who died, and furthermore is also risen, who is even at the right hand of God, who also makes intercession for us.*

*Who shall separate us from the love of Christ? Shall* tribulation, or distress, or persecution, or famine, or nakedness, or peril, or sword?

As it is written: "For Your sake we are killed all day long; We are accounted as sheep for the slaughter." Yet in all these things we are more than conquerors through Him who loved us.

*For I am persuaded that neither death nor life, nor angels nor principalities nor powers, nor things present nor things to come, nor height nor depth, nor any other created thing, shall be able to separate us from the love of God which is in Christ Jesus our Lord."*

There is therefore, no condemnation for those who are in Christ Jesus (Rom. 8:1)! If we are born again, we are joined of the Lord and belong to Him and to His kingdom (I Cor. 6:17). If we judge ourselves according to the flesh, *we are denying the truth of the gospel of grace.* We are practicing the old ways, and as a dog returns to his vomit, so are we if we entangle ourselves in self-recrimination!

We must stop judging ourselves! We are to stop seeing ourselves in the old ways (the old nature), and judging by them. If we judge, we judge ourselves *according to what Christ has done!* Give praise and glory to the forgiveness of sins and the gift of righteousness in Him (Rom. 5:17)! When we judge according to the flesh, we lose our peace. *When we judge according to His righteousness and the Spirit, we stay in peace.*

## Conclusion

Do we judge or not judge? Jesus said not to, but then tells us He judged according to the Spirit. Paul wrote that he who is spiritual judges all things (I Cor. 2:15)! The tension is obvious and the answer is found in affirming both exhortations regarding judging. We are not to judge according to the flesh; we are to judge, as Jesus did, according to the Spirit! Amen.

# CHAPTER XII

# IS GOD TESTING US? DOES GOD PROVE US? OR, DOES GOD CHASTEN US?

Is God testing us or not? Does God chasten us or not? Testing is not the same as chastening; yet, these are related and similar in purpose. The problem begins with definitions because it is easy to combine, mix, and cross over meanings in regards to testing and chastening.

The problem is compounded by the fact that our English translations often use these same words for several Hebrew or Greek words. For example:

> "...you shall not listen to the words of that prophet or that dreamer of dreams, for the LORD your God *is testing you* to know whether you love the LORD your God with all your heart and with all your soul." (Deuteronomy 13:3, emphasis added)

In this passage, the word for *"testing"* is: 05254 נסה nacah naw-saw'

1) To test, try, prove, *tempt*, assay, and put to the proof or test

> "But, O LORD of hosts, You who judge righteously, *testing* the mind and the heart, Let me see Your

vengeance on them, For to You I have revealed my cause." (Jeremiah 11:20, emphasis added)

In this passage, the word for *"testing"* is: 0974 וחַן bachan baw-khan'

1) *To examine, try, prove*

The tension is everywhere as we begin to try to understand what is going on. The theme of this book, the principle, is to stay within the tension scripture reveals about any subject or teaching. A repeated reasoning, when addressing the tension, has been:

1) It's not whether we should judge, but which is the best judgment we should judge with?
2) It's not whether we should suffer, but which is the best suffering we're supposed to suffer in?
3) It's not whether we should progress, but which is the best progression to progress in?

When we apply testing, chastening, even correction, rebuke, instruction, and/or discipline *to the equation (repeated reasoning),* it helps us to discern, focus, and reason properly.

It's not whether we are being tested, but which is the best testing to be tested with? It's not whether we are being chastened, but which is the best chastening to be chastened with? It's not whether we are being corrected, but which is the best correction to be corrected with? It's not whether we are being disciplined, but which is the best discipline to be disciplined with?

The difference between the best and not so best is as different as the Old and New Testaments. The position of the Old Testament man in relationship to God is entirely different than the New Testament man. The problem is that often we have become New Testament born again sons and daughters of God, *only to keep the Old Testament mind set.*

This creates confusion, poor judgment, bad interpretations, and keeps us vulnerable to demonic attacks meant to steal, kill and destroy us. The confusion keeps us in doubt about God's intentions, actions, dealing, and the source behind the things that are happening in our lives. How can we, "Submit to God and resist the devil...? (James 4:7)" if we are not sure what is going on, or who is behind what is happening right now? Is it from God or the enemy?

## It Is a Faith Issue

When we are in confusion and doubt, it is impossible to operate in faith. It is faith that overcomes and has become our victory:

> "For whatever is born of God overcomes the world. And this is the victory that has overcome the world—*our faith.*" (1Jo 5:4, emphasis added)

Many times our faith is weak, or stressed and fearful, and maybe non-existent. Often it is hope. Faith knows God's word. Faith comes from God's Word (Rom. 10:17). Faith is the fruit of the Spirit within us (Gal. 5:22). Faith produces peace, rest, comfort, and knowing. When we understand faith differently from these characteristics, something is wrong.

How do we know these characteristics of faith? We know them from God's word; especially from understanding what the apostle James wrote:

> "If any of you lacks wisdom, let him ask of God, who gives to all liberally and without reproach, and it will be given to him.
> *But let him ask in faith, with no doubting,* for he who doubts is like a wave of the sea driven and tossed by the wind.

For let not that man suppose that he will receive anything from the Lord; *he is a double-minded man, unstable in all his ways."* (James 1: 5-8, emphasis added)

This passage has become quite a powerful source for understanding faith. From this passage, we learn that faith is not doubting; therefore, faith is single minded as opposed to double minded. Faith is stable, as opposed to unstable. We learn that faith knows God's will, while doubt doesn't. Doubt is double minded, being tossed back and forth like the waves of the sea. Doubt is caught between two or more opinions about what God's will is.

When it comes to understanding testing, chastening, correction, rebuke, and discipline, so many of us are tossed back and forth; we are in doubt. We don't know if what is coming our way is from God or from the enemy. Are the troubles, problems, obstacles, stresses, worries, persecutions, sicknesses, and/or setbacks, happening right now in our lives, from God or from the enemy? Not knowing the answer to this question puts us in doubt. It puts us in the wrong tension too, the tension of doubt. As a point of clarity, ask this question, "Did Jesus live in doubt?"

When Jesus said or taught these things, we need to discern (remember) what is going on, with emphasis added:

"...and they have no root in themselves, and so endure only for a time.
Afterward, when tribulation or persecution arises *for the word's sake,* immediately they stumble.
Now these are the ones sown among thorns; they are the ones who hear the word, and the cares of this world, the deceitfulness of riches, and the desires for other things *entering in choke the word,* and it becomes unfruitful." (Mr 4:17-19)

"These things I have spoken to you, that in Me you may have peace. *In the world you will have tribulation; but be of good cheer, I have overcome the world."* (Joh 16:33)

> *"The thief does not come except to steal, and to kill, and*
> *to destroy. I have come that they may have life, and that*
> *they may have it more abundantly."* (Joh 10:10)

In the *Parable of the Seed and the Sower*, Jesus teaches us that the word of God is being stolen from, persecuted, competed against, and choked out. Certainly, we can all grasp that these efforts are not from God. Furthermore, Jesus said that the world itself is filled with tribulation.

> *Tribulation* (θλῖψις thlipsis thlip'-sis.) means or contains
> these things: tribulation, affliction, and trouble, and
> anguish, persecution, burdened, to be afflicted...
> 1) *A pressing, pressing together, pressure*

Jesus said we are to be of good cheer, because He overcame the world; however, if we do not discern properly, we are going to be accepting things into our lives for which He overcame. Also, in our confusion, we may attribute to God things coming against us that are of this world. He overcame sickness and disease in His atonement (Isa. 53:5 & 2 Pet. 2:24); He redeemed us from the curse of the law (Gal. 3:13)! If or when, we accept sickness or disease into our life as from God, something is wrong again. God isn't going to chastise us with the curse of the law if Jesus redeemed us from it.

Under the Old Testament, God did use sickness and disease, and He used the curse of the law, to chastise, rebuke, reprove, and correct the children of Israel, because He had to. We are born of God, and stand as sons and daughters with the Holy Spirit within us, to teach, guide, strengthen, instruct, admonish, convict, and/or correct.

If we accept things coming against us as from God to teach, instruct, chasten, reprove, test, or discipline us, when they are coming from the world (the enemy or the curse), we are in the wrong place: vulnerable, and being stolen from. Bless God, because of His mercy and almighty power, He is able to take all these things, the good, bad, and evil things, and turn them for our good (Rom. 8:28). This doesn't mean He wants us to submit to these things; but if we do, He is able to turn evil around for our good. His promise in the word is this:

> *"And the Lord will deliver me from every evil work* and preserve me for His heavenly kingdom. To Him be glory forever and ever. Amen!" (2Ti 4:18, emphasis added)

## Two Opposing Sides

The third verse (John 10:10) I presented speaks about two opposing sides in this world full of tribulation. The thief comes to steal, kill, and destroy; Jesus came to give us abundant life (John 10:10). We need to know how the thief comes against us to do these things. According to the *Parable of the Seed and the Sower*, it is through stealing, taking away, persecuting, competing against, and choking the word out from our hearts.

The Word of God in the New Testament includes these themes, with emphasis added:

> "If you endure *chastening,* God deals with you as with sons; for what son is there whom a father does not chasten?" (Heb 12:7)

> "As many as I love, *I rebuke and chasten.* Therefore be zealous and repent." (Re 3:19)

> "Because you have kept My command to persevere, I also will keep you from the *hour of trial* which shall come upon the whole world, *to test those who dwell on the earth."* (Re 3:10)

> "For to this end I also wrote *that I might put you to the test,* whether you are obedient in all things." (2Co 2:9)

"Examine yourselves as to whether you are in the faith. *Test yourselves.* Do you not know yourselves that Jesus Christ is in you?—unless indeed you are disqualified." (2Co 13:5)

"*Test all things*; hold fast what is good." (1Th 5:21)

"*...knowing that the testing of your faith* produces patience." (Jas 1:3)

"*Others, testing Him,* sought from Him a sign from heaven." (Lu 11:16)

"This they said, *testing Him,* that they might have something of which to accuse Him. But Jesus stooped down and wrote on the ground with His finger, as though He did not hear." (Joh 8:6)

"Jesus said to him, 'It is written again, '*You shall not tempt the LORD your God.*'" (Mt 4:7, {#De 6:16})

"*...nor let us tempt Christ,* as some of them also tempted, and were destroyed by serpents..." (1Co 10:9)

"Let no one say when he is tempted, '*I am tempted by God*'; for God cannot be tempted by evil, nor does He Himself tempt anyone." (Jas 1:13)

This list of verses represent the tension we all face when trying to discern which is the best chastening, testing, discipline, and even trials, we are to accept from God.

In the Old Testament, when God had to deal with humanity from the outside (not the heart), His efforts to test them were external as well. God could not speak, prompt, chastise, correct, or instruct from the heart and inner man.

The people did not have the Spirit born within them; therefore, when God spoke it was discipline, correction, chastisement, and rebuke coming from outside of their being. The word of God, the Law of Moses, the commands and precepts, all of it was like fences to unregenerate souls. Along with this condition, the fact that sinners do not understand the things of God, respect or appreciate spiritual things (I Cor. 2:14), means they had to be related to through naturalism—what they could see, hear, feel, touch, taste, or smell, through their senses.

The natural man is sense driven, carnal, and physically dependent. Like animals, human beings had to be tested, chastened, corrected, and disciplined physically. Old Testament people had to be *corralled*. Quite frankly, God could do no better with them than to deal with their natural condition. At that time, no hearts could be changed; all were spiritually dead (disconnected) to God.

This meant that God's testing: chastening, rebuke, correction, and discipline had to involve physical applications.

> "Then the LORD said to Moses, "Behold, I will rain bread from heaven for you. And the people shall go out and gather a certain quota every day, *that I may test them,* whether they will walk in My law or not." (Ex 16:4, emphasis added)

> "O LORD, are not Your eyes on the truth? *You have stricken them,* but they have not grieved; *You have consumed them,* But they have refused to receive correction. They have made their faces harder than rock; they have refused to return." (Jer 5:3, emphasis added)

> "So you shall say to them, '*This is a nation that does not obey the voice of the LORD their God nor receive correction.* Truth has perished and has been cut off from their mouth.'" (Jer 7:28, emphasis added)

God had to deal with humanity with physical discipline. He had to rebuke them with the sword, defeat (Lev. 26:17), sickness and disease, famine, plague, and natural calamities. He could not change their hearts, so He had to deal with their *flesh*. It is very important to realize that God had to deal with them according to their sin nature:

> "Then, if you walk contrary to Me, and are not willing to obey Me, *I will bring on you seven times more plagues, according to your sins.*" (Le 26:21, emphasis added)

> "Then the anger of the LORD was aroused against this land, *to bring on it every curse that is written in this book.*" (De 29:27, emphasis added)

In a way, it is like dealing with evil. Evil only recognizes power, not negotiation, not reason, but physical power. It was not God's will, but because of the condition of man, He had to work with them from the outside.

> *"Do not be like the horse or like the mule,* which have no understanding, which must be harnessed with bit and bridle, Else they will not come near you." (Ps 32:9

Under the New Testament, after the resurrection of Christ and when the Holy Spirit was sent into our hearts, this all changed. God can operate in New Testament people with grace through the Spirit; He works from the inside now.

We know the Lord! We have His divine nature born into us (I John 3:9); we can know His will, and by the power of the Holy Spirit, live in it and fulfill it. The difference is night and day.

> "I beseech you therefore, brethren, by the mercies of God, that you present your bodies a living sacrifice, holy, acceptable to God, which is your reasonable service.
> And do not be conformed to this world, *but be transformed by the renewing of your mind, that you may prove what is that good and acceptable and perfect will of God.*" (Rom. 12: 1, 2, emphasis added)

113

We are able to be led, not by a harness and bit, but by the Spirit:

> "For as many as are *led by the Spirit of God*, these are sons of God." (Ro 8:14, emphasis added)

This is huge! Now, God speaks to our hearts to instruct, to lead, to correct, to admonish, to teach, to instruct, and to discipline! He was forced under the Old Testament to bring physical things to bear in order to correct, rebuke, lead, and corral. Under the new situation, His word rebukes, corrects, leads, and corrals from the inside out! Read this again:

> "*All Scripture* is given by inspiration of God, and is *profitable for doctrine, for reproof, for correction, for instruction in righteousness, that the man of God may be complete*, thoroughly equipped for every good work." (2Ti 3:16, 17, emphasis added)

## What About Chastening?

Let me revisit some New Testament verses with this new creation understanding: "It's not whether we are chastened by the Lord, but which chastening is the best chastening to be chastened with (emphasis added)."

> "If you endure **chastening**, God deals with you as with sons; for what son is there whom a father does not chasten?" (Heb 12:7)

And,

> "As many as I love, *I rebuke and chasten*. Therefore be zealous and repent." (Re 3:19)

If we keep the Old Testament understanding of "chastening," we are going to be scriptural, but will we be rightly dividing the word of truth? Will we be standing in the new creation, the New Testament, and in His grace?

> "But *if you are led by the Spirit, you are not under the law."* (Ga 5:18)

Under the Old Testament, everyone was under the law! It is the curse of the Law that brings about so much suffering on the earth; furthermore, it was the curse of the Law that God had to use to corral the unregenerate.

If we read Moses' writing in Deuteronomy chapter 28, we'd see a lengthy list of curses. These curses were to come upon the Children of Israel for *disobedience*. It was the power of the curse (of the law) that is also affirmed in the New Testament:

> "The sting of death is sin; *and the strength of sin is the law."* (I Cor. 15: 56, emphasis added)

Under the law, God dealt with everyone according to their own works. This is also confirmed in the New Testament:

> *"Do not be deceived,* God is not mocked; *for whatever a man sows, that he will also reap.*
> *For he who sows to his flesh will of the flesh reap corruption, but he who sows to the Spirit will of the Spirit reap everlasting life."* (Gal. 6:7, 8, emphasis added)

Under the New Testament, we have an amazing option: we can receive from God the new creation realities or continue to live under the law. We can begin to receive, by faith, the rights of the new kingdom (Col. 1:13), or remain under the old. In other words, God will deal with us according to how Christ fulfilled the law and finished the race. Or, He may reluctantly have to continue to deal with us under the law. This is not His will; but rather that we'd stand in, assert, and walk in the Spirit. We get to exchange places with Him by living in faith by His grace:

"For He made Him who knew no sin to be sin for us, *that we might become the righteousness of God in Him.*" (2Co 5:21, emphasis added)

## An Illustration May Help:

God having to deal with us according to the law is like having to communicate with us through the noise of a crowd. Think of two people calling across the room in a crowed party: The noise of the room makes it difficult to hear and comprehend. It's easy confusing the meaning of what is being said. It is cumbersome, froth with interference, and very difficult to confirm what is being communicated. The two could easily misunderstand each other.

God dealing with us through being born again is even better than two people in a quiet place, sitting next to each other: speaking, confirming, and reassuring each other of their meaning. They would have opportunity to clarify, reconnect, and eliminate confusion. God's Spirit is joined with our spirit in the inner man (I Cor. 6:17). His peace, His word, His joy, His rest, and His assurance can by-pass all of the interference of the world.

Sowing and reaping are still sovereign in this world; however, we get to decide whether we sow to the flesh or to the Spirit. This option not only changes our position from being slaves and servants of the law to sons and daughters, it also intimately changes how God leads, guides, instructs, empowers, and dwells in us.

It fundamentally changes how God deals with us! To chasten people under the Old Testament, He had to do so from the outside, with physical manifestations, often through the curse. To chasten us under the New Testament, He only has to speak, prompt, instruct, lead, and guide us from His word by the Spirit within. In short, He had to use the curse (among other things) to corral them under the Old situation; under the New, He uses His relationship to us in Christ. They were led by the Law and circumstances; we are led by the Spirit and His word of grace!

When New Testament people remain under the Old Testament status and operation, we are missing grace!

> *"Let the word of Christ dwell in you richly* in all wisdom, *teaching and admonishing* one another in psalms and hymns and spiritual songs, singing with grace in your hearts to the Lord." (Col 3:16, emphasis added)

We are to be led by the Spirit in His peace! Let the peace of God instruct, correct, rebuke, and reprove us!

> *"And let the peace of God rule in your hearts,* to which also you were called in one body; and be thankful." (Col 3:15, emphasis added)

## What About "Testing?"

Here are New Testament verses dealing with "testing (emphasis added):"

> *"Others, testing Him,* sought from Him a sign from heaven." (Lu 11:16)

> "This they said, *testing Him,* that they might have something of which to accuse Him. But Jesus stooped down and wrote on the ground with His finger, as though He did not hear." (Joh 8:6)

> "For to this end I also wrote *that I might put you to the test,* whether you are obedient in all things." (2Co 2:9)

> "Examine yourselves as to whether you are in the faith. *Test yourselves.* Do you not know yourselves that Jesus Christ is in you?—unless indeed you are disqualified." (2Co 13:5)

> *"Test all things;* hold fast what is good." (1Th 5:21)

*"...knowing that the testing of your faith* produces patience." (Jas 1:3)

"Because you have kept My command to persevere, I also will keep you from the *hour of trial* which shall come upon the whole world, *to test those who dwell on the earth."* (Re 3:10)

The first few verses refer to the "testing" *of* Jesus. This testing was from men towards Jesus. They were trying to trap Him into saying something wrong. They wanted to force Him into complying, cooperating, and subjugating Himself to their influence. This kind of testing is common to all. We have called it peer pressure, following the crowd, succumbing to popular opinion, the fear of man, combating the "establishment" of government, or appeasing the powerful and influential.

None of these types of testing are coming from God towards us—especially for the born again believer. These tests were antagonistic in purpose, for the world's agenda, rather than God's call upon Jesus.

This testing reminds us of Jesus rebuking Peter:

"But when He had turned around and looked at His disciples, He rebuked Peter, saying, *'Get behind Me, Satan! For you are not mindful of the things of God, but the things of men.'"* (Mr 8:33, emphasis added)

The next three verses were written by Paul in his epistles (2 Cor. 2:9, 2 Cor. 13:5, I Thes. 5:21). The testing Paul puts forth in these verses has to do with human examination towards *spiritual things*. The first of the three, Paul writes to challenge, test, prove, and reveal, to see if they "are obedient in all things." God inspired Paul to put forth this test. It is a tool to help determine our heart's condition towards spiritual life. Our willingness to obey reflects which nature is dominating us.

God already knows what actually the case is; we are often the ones that don't realize what is going on. The test, therefore, is to help us see, sift through deceptions, and then focus on spiritual things. God's test through Paul is purposed to awaken us to righteousness:

> "*Awake to righteousness*, and do not sin; for some do not have the knowledge of God. I speak this to your shame." (1Co 15:34, emphasis added)

The test itself is based solely upon the Word of God. It is based in the Spirit of God. It is an internal examination that is reflected in outward signs of obedience. God is communicating to us from within our own hearts and conscious mind. It is to stir Christ consciousness within us so that we'll walk after the Spirit:

> "I say then: *Walk in the Spirit and you shall not fulfill the lust of the flesh.*" (Ga 5:16, emphasis added)

The next two types of tests presented: "test yourselves" and "test all things" are similar spiritual disciplines. The first is to examine our own heart and to stand in our salvation in Christ. Self examination is absolutely from God, *but is subject to us.* It is for our benefit. It is our need to know where we are in relationship to God's plan of salvation. *The key, however, is to examine ourselves according to the Spirit, not the flesh!*

The second examination is referring to what this book is about. We are to test all things, to recognize whether they are from God or not. We are to test the scriptures with the scriptures, to discern the truth. The tension that is in the scriptures is itself a test.

*When we deny scripture to stand in scripture, something is skewed. When we deny revelation to find revelation, something is missing.* It is when we remain in the tension that we find truth, guidance, safety, and amazing revelations of the Holy Spirit.

The purpose of these self-examining tests is for our good. These are the good tests we should be testing ourselves with. Is

God sending these tests? He is indeed, but they come through the inner spiritual life birthed into us when we became born again. He wants us to be sober minded, watchful, testing the spirits, and examining all things by His Word and Spirit dwelling within us. Amen.

## Testing of Your Faith

The next two verses actually address the thrust of this chapter. Does God test our faith? Does God reprove it? Is God examining our faith in order to approve it?

> "...*knowing that the testing of your faith* produces patience." (Jas 1:3, emphasis added)

Here is the context surrounding this verse:

> "My brethren, *count it all joy when you fall into various trials*, knowing that the testing of your faith produces patience.
> *But let patience have its perfect work*, that you may be perfect and complete, lacking nothing." (James 1:2-4, emphasis added)

The major question regarding this passage is, "Who is testing our faith?" Is God bringing the trials in order to test our faith? Or, is it the world, the curse of the law, and the enemy of our faith, bringing the test? How we decide to answer these questions matters.

Jesus said:

> "These things I have spoken to you, that in Me you may have peace. *In the world you will have tribulation; but be of good cheer, I have overcome the world.*" (Joh 16:33, emphasis added)

In this world, we'll have tribulations coming against us; but, be of good cheer, because Jesus has overcome the world. This makes it clear that the tribulations are not coming from God, or Jesus would have been overcoming God. With this understanding, then James chapter one makes better sense: God is not testing our faith; the world is.

The world is coming against us because we are no longer of this world (John 18:36). We were once in darkness and children of it, but now, we are sons and daughters of the light in the Lord (Eph. 5:8). We are of a new and better kingdom. The opposing force is not God; it is the fallen world, the curse of the law upon sinners, and the devil.

Why should we consider it all joy when trials come against us? Jesus said we should be of, "good cheer" because He overcame the world. Furthermore, He then turns to us and says:

> "Behold, *I give you the authority* to trample on serpents and scorpions, and *over all the power of the enemy,* and nothing shall by any means hurt you." (Lu 10:19, emphasis added)

Count it all joy because we are no longer *mere* men under the curse of the law, and subject to the elements of this world (Gal. 4:3). Count it all joy because we've been given the gift of righteousness and with it we reign with Christ:

> "For if by the one man's offense death reigned through the one, much more those who receive abundance of grace *and of the gift of righteousness will reign in life through the One, Jesus Christ."* (Rom. 5:17, emphasis added)

The testing going on in this situation is not God trying to prove us, examine, or rebuke us through trials. It is not God trying to strengthen our faith and improve our patience, thereby, building our character. Rather, it is the world trying to tear down our faith (the enemy through the world). *How do we know this?*

We know this because God would not be coming against us with things Jesus overcame. We know this because trials and tribulations are from this world:

> *"Woe to the world because of offenses!* For offenses must come, *but woe to that man by whom the offense comes!"* (Mt 18:7, emphasis added)

God is not going to bring trials, tribulations, and offenses into our life when Jesus opposed them, overcame them, and condemned them. God and Jesus are on the same side:

> "If a kingdom is divided against itself, *that kingdom cannot stand."* (Mr 3:24, emphasis added)

Further, patience is at work in this passage for our good. Whose patience is it? Is it our human patience? No, it is the fruit of the Spirit working in us to do the will of God (Phip. 2:13). God's patience is working in us, for we are His workmanship created in Christ Jesus for good works (Eph. 2:10). We let God's patience work in us to reveal the full nature of the new creation, when facing trials.

It is important to realize something at this point. Under the Old Testament, God was outside of His people, having to deal with them from a distance. He was observing, aiding, corralling, and working in their lives as an outside "force." *He was not the only force involved in their lives.* We could say He was one among many. This also means that when trials came against them in Old Testament conditions, they were on their own. They had no comforter:

> "Then I returned and considered all the oppression that is done under the sun: And look! The tears of the oppressed, *But they have no comforter--On the side of their oppressors there is power, But they have no comforter."* (Ec 4:1, emphasis added)

Under the New Testament condition, God is with us, inside of us, *helping us oppose the forces coming against us!* The Holy Spirit is our comforter! He is our Helper (John 15:26)! When tests, trials, and tribulations come our away because of the world, God is with us against them!

> "What then shall we say to these things? *If God is for us, who can be against us?*" (Ro 8:31, emphasis added)

Or:

> *"You are of God, little children, and have overcome them, because He who is in you is greater than he who is in the world."* (1Jo 4:4, emphasis added)

We are never alone, God will never forsake us or leave us, and He is with us to deliver us (Heb. 13:5)! Count it all joy because we have God who is our help in times of trouble (Ps. 9:9)! Count it all joy because we are helped (2 Cor. 2:6)!

It is like taking a final exam for an important class, but we are not alone. God is actually sitting in the chair with us, helping us to overcome. We can do all things through Christ, who strengthens us!

> *"I can do all things through Christ* who strengthens me." (Php 4:13, emphasis added)

## What about Temptations?

Temptations, tempting, to tempt, are also related to testing, chastening, correcting, rebuking, and disciplining, in the Christian life.

Here is the meaning surrounding to tempt (From the Old and New Testament words):

*To test, try, prove, tempt, assay, put to the proof or test, to test one maliciously, craftily to put to the proof his feelings or judgments, by enticement to sin.*

Who is tempting? We know evil tempts us to sin. We know people entice us to sin. Our own sinful desires lure us to sin (James 1:4). Would God tempt us? Would God put us to the test, to prove our worth, to craftily seek to pressure us in order to show what we are made of? God already knows our status and sin condition. Look at these verses (emphasis added); they seem to say something directly about this last question I pose:

"Jesus said to him, 'It is written again, *'You shall not tempt the LORD your God.'*" (Mt 4:7, {#De 6:16})

"*...nor let us tempt Christ,* as some of them also tempted, and were destroyed by serpents..." (1Co 10:9)

"Let no one say when he is tempted, *"I am tempted by God"; for God cannot be tempted by evil, nor does He Himself tempt anyone."* (Jas 1:13)

God doesn't tempt anyone. That is pretty straightforward. This would mean that God doesn't provoke, incite, tempt, or seek to solicit evil desires from us; at the same time, God isn't provoked, incited, or tempted, nor can someone solicit evil desire from Him (contrary to the account of Job). Jesus said something rather intriguing about this:

"I will no longer talk much with you, *for the ruler of this world is coming, and he has nothing in Me.*" (Joh 14:30, emphasis added)

In the divine nature, there is nothing to tempt. When we became born again, that same nature became our nature (I John 4:7). We have the same nature in us because we are born of God!

Therefore, in our new creation realities, we cannot be provoked, incited, tempted, or solicited to do evil. When we are tempted, incited, provoked, and lured into evil with sinful passions to fall, it is our old nature we are living to.

God is not going to tempt us, test us, or prove us, in order to establish in us *what He has already given to us!* We were given all things that pertain to life and godliness (2 Pet. 1:3)! We don't need character development; we need to become *aware* of the character of Christ given to us! Let this character become *more influential* in our lives by living to the Spirit. We don't need to become more like Christ, *we have Christ*; we need to become more *aware, confident, and bold in Christ!*

## Conclusion:

God is not sending through the world tests, trials, temptations, corrections, and rebukes, against us as born again sons and daughters. This is because He has access to our hearts through the Spirit within us. He doesn't have to corral us in the midst of the interference, noise, and clamor of this world's tribulations. He can speak, lead, and guide us from within through His peace, His word, His joy, and His love. We are already in our spirit man, just as He is (I John 4:7). This certainly emphasizes our need to be in prayer always (I Th. 5:17):

> *"My sheep hear My voice, and I know them, and they follow Me."* (Joh 10:27, emphasis added)

God is not sending, or using the ways He had to use in the Old Testament conditions; in contrast, He is now within us, *helping us to face the tests*, trials, temptations, and tribulations that are coming against us to steal, kill, and destroy the word in our hearts.

God is not testing our faith, because He gave us the *faith of Christ* (Gal. 2:20). He doesn't need to reprove us, because we have the very nature and character of Christ—He is our life (Col. 3:4)!

God doesn't need to discipline us through trials and troubles, like He did the Old Testament people, because we are now joined in one Spirit with the Lord (I Cor. 6:7). If we need correcting, His Spirit, His Word, His peace, and His love communicate within our hearts what needs to be corrected. God now leads us from the inside, helping us confront the forces coming against us on the outside.

The battle we face, He faces with us. The battle rages within our heart and mind, so put on the mind of Christ! The battle is being fought over what we believe and what we'll stand in. It is being fought to keep us grace minded. It is being fought over what we accept or resist. It is being fought within us to acknowledge, stand, and assert the truth brought to us in Jesus (Philemon 1:6). It is not whether we are to be tested or chastened; it is which is the best testing, and best chastening, we are to engage in.

We stand in His righteousness, we stand in His stead, we are to submit to God and resist the devil. We are to walk in faith by His grace. We need to know God's will, and be able to discern what is from God and what is from this world.

> "For 'who has known the mind of the LORD that He may instruct him?' *But we have the mind of Christ.*" (1Co 2:16, emphasis added)

## The Tribulation Is a World Wide Test

The final verse listed concerns the Tribulation Period that is coming upon the earth. This is the time of great trial when the antichrist will be given, or take full human power, to rule and reign for a short period of time:

> "Because you have kept My command to persevere, I also will keep you from the *hour of trial* which shall come upon the whole world, *to test those who dwell on the earth.*" (Re 3:10, emphasis added)

The testing is God allowing man to have what they deserve. It is God taking away the restraining influence of the Spirit (2 Thes. 2:7). It is God's wrath upon unrepentant, rebellious, and obstinate people. The test is justice prevailing among sinful and deluded people. It is the demonic being free to dominate selfishness upon the earth.

Is God bringing the test? Hardly, it is God finally allowing man to have his way (stepping away); a way that will be dominated by evil and evil spirits. It is also a time when God's wrath will be poured out upon all flesh. In regards to saints, the rapture will take all of us out of the way before this time (I Cor. 15:52), and as a result of our departure, the restraining will be gone.

# CHAPTER XIII

# WORKS AND FAITH: WHAT IS GOING ON BETWEEN THEM?

Whole divides exist in the Christian world over our understanding of works and faith, of works and God's grace. The divide between Protestism and Roman Catholicism centers a great deal over how works and faith are applied, taught, and interpreted from scripture.

*Martin Luther's* declarative statement, "Justification through faith alone," was a shot across the bow of Roman Catholicism. The Roman Church had emphasized works as proof of salvation, and with it a standard of marks that were to be kept from womb to tomb (Christening, First Communion, Catechism, Confession, The Mass, Last Rites, etc.). It was proclaimed by some powerful forces within the Roman Catholic Church that there is no salvation outside of the church.

This meant that what the Roman Church declared, required, and practiced, was mandatory upon all adherents to the Christian faith. The rituals, regulations, and laws of the church, established, maintained, and measured one's salvation status. To fall out of grace with the Roman Church, and to be excommunicated, meant certain damnation and the curse of Hell. It held sway for nearly twelve-hundred years—until the Reformation.

When the Roman Catholic powers of that day responded to the Reformation, and especially to Martin Luther's "faith alone" stance, they labeled him a heretic. They accused him of being against the law and the commandments. They coined a phrase, "Antinomianism," which was referring to someone who had rejected the law and moral constraints upon the people. They argued that Martin Luther was teaching the people to live unrestrained lives. His response then became:

> "We are justified by faith alone *but not by a faith that is alone.*" (Essential Truths of the Faith, p. 191)

The conflict arises from the tension found in the testimony of scripture! There are verses that put heavy conditions upon our salvation, and there are verses that completely remove them. Are we saved by faith alone in what Jesus did, or are we saved by works that accompany it?

Let me present both sides of this tension, works and faith, from the following scriptures (emphasis added):

## Is Salvation By Works (Or Conditions)?

> "When He had called the people to Himself, with His disciples also, He said to them, *'Whoever desires to come after Me, let him deny himself, and take up his cross, and follow Me.'*" (Mr 8:34)

> "*He who loves father or mother more than Me is not worthy of Me.* And he who loves son or daughter more than Me is not worthy of Me." (Mt 10:37)

> "So likewise, whoever of you *does not forsake all that he has cannot be My disciple.*" (Lu 14:33)

> "But Jesus said to him, *'No one, having put his hand to the plow, and looking back, is fit for the kingdom of God.'*" (Lu 9:62)

"Jesus said to him, '*You shall love the LORD your God with all your heart, with all your soul, and with all your mind.*'" (Mt 22:37)

"But do you want to know, O foolish man, *that faith without works is dead?*" (Jas 2:20)

## These Verses Point to Our Works as Meaning Nothing, it is Faith in Christ (emphasis added):

"I am the vine, you are the branches. He who abides in Me, and I in him, bears much fruit; *for without Me you can do nothing.*" (Joh 15:5)

"For by grace you have been saved through faith, *and that not of yourselves; it is the gift of God, not of works, lest anyone should boast.*
*For we are His workmanship,* created in Christ Jesus for good works, which God prepared beforehand that we should walk in them." (Eph. 2: 8-10)

"This only I want to learn from you: *Did you receive the Spirit by the works of the law, or by the hearing of faith?*" (Ga 3:2)

"Therefore *He is also able to save to the uttermost* those who come to God through Him, since He always lives to make intercession for them." (Heb 7:25)

"For if by one man's offence death reigned by one; much more they which receive abundance of grace *and of the gift of righteousness shall reign in life by one, Jesus Christ.*" (Rom. 5:17)

"*But that no one is justified by the law in the sight of God is evident, for "the just shall live by faith."* (Ga 3:11)

It is really any wonder that we struggle to see clearly what salvation is dependent upon? We have a clear conflict, a tension within scripture, about salvation having conditions (works) or it being settled in faith alone. Especially since the words of Christ Himself include strenuous conditions!

Who among us can love God with all our heart? Who among us can deny him/her self to follow Him? Who can forsake all that he or she has to be found worthy enough? Who among us has put our hand to the plow of serving God and has not looked back? If we are honest, these conditions put us in a precarious position of wondering if we are doing enough. Are we loving God enough, denying ourselves enough, or staying faithful in our service enough?

If these conditions are true, who can be saved? If Jesus placed these burdens upon us for us to keep, what genuine peace do we have? There is, however, another way to understand what Jesus was teaching. We can come to this conclusion, if we allow the tension of these apparently opposing views of scripture on salvation to remain.

## The Old Testament Law and Jesus

Consider this truth: Jesus had to teach the law in ways that made it clear it is impossible to keep. He did this because the Jewish leaders were teaching the people that the Law of Moses could be kept. When the religious leaders taught the law, it wasn't taught in its purity, which includes the spirit of the matter.

For example, the Jewish leaders would teach the commandment, "Thou shalt not commit adultery." Jesus taught the commandment to its full penetration, reflecting upon the spiritual condition. The commandment was meant to expose the inward sin nature of sinners, so He said, "Anyone who looks upon a woman to lust after her, commits adultery in his heart."

When Jesus teaches us to deny ourselves, to forsake all that we have, to pick up our cross daily, and then love God more than even our lives, He is doing the same thing. He is expanding upon the true nature of God's requirements upon us. God is not doing this to see if we can do it; He is doing this to show us we can't!

The purpose of the law was to bring to light the sin problem. The law's purpose, as Paul wrote in 2 Cor. 3:6-9, with emphasis added, is this:

> "...who also made us sufficient as ministers of the new covenant, not of the letter but of the Spirit; *for the letter kills,* but the Spirit gives life. *But if the ministry of death, written and engraved on stones,* was glorious, so that the children of Israel could not look steadily at the face of Moses because of the glory of his countenance, which glory was passing away, how will the ministry of the Spirit not be more glorious? *For if the ministry of condemnation had glory,* the ministry of righteousness exceeds much more in glory.

And Paul succinctly said:

> "Therefore by the deeds of the law no flesh will be justified in His sight, *for by the law is the knowledge of sin.*" (Ro 3:20)

These two verses, and there are more, show us that the purpose of the law was to expose sin. It was to bring condemnation upon all works of self righteousness! The law was a ministry of death to us! It was our tutor to reveal our incurable condition, so that we would readily turn to the savior:

> "Therefore *the law was our tutor to bring us to Christ,* that we might be justified by faith." (Ga 3:24, emphasis added)

When Jesus went to the cross, atonement was made for all sin. He fulfilled the law's requirements against us:

> *"And you, being dead in your trespasses* and the uncircumcision of your flesh, He has made alive together with Him, *having forgiven you all trespasses, having wiped out the handwriting of requirements that was against us, which was contrary to us.*
> *And He has taken it out of the way, having nailed it to the cross.*
> *Having disarmed principalities and powers, He made a public spectacle of them, triumphing over them in it."* (Col. 2: 13-15, emphasis added)

He has taken judgment out of the way by fulfilling it from the law against us. We are no longer under the law's judgments, we are under grace:

> "For sin shall not have dominion over you, *for you are not under law but under grace."* (Ro 6:14, emphasis added)

Therefore, we do not walk by sight, works, or our own righteousness, but by faith in His grace. We walk by what He accomplished and finished in the cross! We died to sin; we now live to Christ who has become our life. Jesus also said:

> *"...for without Me you can do nothing."* (John 15: 5, emphasis added)

We have nothing to offer without Him. We can do nothing without Him. We are saved completely by the work of salvation in Jesus (Heb. 7:25). We can't add one thing to it. We were lost in sin, totally depraved of His divine nature; however, in the new creation we've been made complete, born of His nature, and given the gift of righteousness (Rom. 5:17). We can do all things through Christ who strengthens us (Phip. 4:13).

## Jesus Gives Paul the Update!

The New Testament epistles, especially Paul's revelations, remove the law's burden upon us because Jesus fulfilled the law for us. Jesus reveals to Paul that the atonement changes everything! We are no longer under the law's judgment and have passed from death to life in the new creation (2 Cor. 5:17). The law is for sinners; grace is for saints! We don't do away with the law and become lawless; we actually live to Jesus, and therefore, we have fulfilled it. The law becomes unnecessary to us because Christ is far more to us than the law could ever be! The law cannot change hearts, Jesus does:

> "...that the righteous requirement of the law *might be fulfilled in us who do not walk according to the flesh but according to the Spirit."* (Ro 8:4, emphasis added)

When we walk according to the Spirit in faith, we automatically kick in a new gear and the new creation realities! When we look to Jesus, relate to Him, and let the peace of God rule in our hearts, we automatically live through the divine nature in us to the things that please the Lord. Jesus saved us from our sin nature, and He saves us to the uttermost through His intercession (Heb. 7:25). We stand in Him; He is our life.

If we walk after the Spirit, we will not fulfill the lusts of the flesh. When we relate to Jesus, we don't have to relate to regulations, rules, or commands—they become obsolete.

## An Illustration

Our dogs don't run away. We let them out to do their business every day and night. They will do their rounds about the yard, they will sit in the sun, and when other dogs walk by, they bark from their own yard. They don't leave. This means they do not need a fence.

Other dogs are not like this. If they are let out, they run. Many dog owners need a fence to keep their dogs home. A fence is needed for a dog that goes astray and goes its own way. A fence is not needed for a dog, which by its own nature, stays home.

Likewise, for the born again believer, Jesus is our life. We have a new nature that does not sin:

> "Whoever *has been born of God does not sin, for His seed remains in him; and he cannot sin,* because he has been born of God." (1Jo 3:9, emphasis added)

The born again believer does not need a fence if he or she is living to Jesus. Having said this, it means we don't need the law, to be judged by it or try to keep it, as in good works. The old measure and standard of good works is dead—the outward version. We have Christ, and His life in us produces good fruit, makes us productive, and useful. We live by faith in Jesus, walking in His grace.

## Faith without Works?

Yet, James, the apostle, wrote:

> "But someone will say, 'You have faith, and I have works.' *Show me your faith without your works, and I will show you my faith by my works.*" (Jas 2:18, emphasis added)

And then continues with,

> "But do you want to know, O foolish man, *that faith without works is dead?*" (Jas. 2:20, emphasis added)

We are saved by grace through faith in what Jesus did; yet, there are works we must do. These works show our faith! There are works involved *with* salvation. Our faith and works should agree. The question becomes, is our salvation dependent upon these works? The answer is no; however, for us to be fruitful for God's kingdom in this earth, there are works we are predestined to do:

> *"For we are His workmanship,* created in Christ Jesus for good works, *which God prepared beforehand that we should walk in them."* (Eph 2:10, emphasis added)

The tension is created because, although we are saved by faith in His grace, our faith is not alone! Our salvation faith, the gift of the Spirit, works in and through us to produce fruits of righteousness. These works are not our own, they are manifestations of the Spirit working in us. Jesus said:

> "Do you not believe that I am in the Father, and the Father in Me? The words that I speak to you I do not speak on My own authority; *but the Father who dwells in Me does the works."* (Joh 14:10, emphasis added)

It is not whether we are to do works, but which are the best works to be working in? It is self righteousness and human works that are unacceptable to God. No one can boast in His presence, or take credit for anything we have done.

> "But we are all like an unclean thing, *and all our righteousnesses are like filthy rags;* we all fade as a leaf, and our iniquities, like the wind, Have taken us away." (Isa 64:6, emphasis added)

## The Right Works of Righteousness

What are the works James speaks about? What are the works that Jesus is referring to that the "Father who dwells in me does the works?"

There is a good saying that helps discern the answer to questions like these: "We don't work *for* our salvation; we work *because* of it." No one is justified, saved, or found worthy of salvation by our own works. No one can keep the law:

> "For as many as are of the works of the law are under the curse; for it is written, *'Cursed is everyone who does not continue in all things which are written in the book of the law,* to do them.'" (Ga 3:10, emphasis added)

James also witnessed:

> "For whoever shall keep the whole law, *and yet stumble in one point, he is guilty of all.*" (Jas 2:10, emphasis added)

These verses, when kept in the tension of the whole counsel of God's word, make us look deeper. We must think and meditate upon things in a more developed perspective, which only occurs while we affirm the scriptures on both sides. How can salvation be only by faith in His grace, but faith must also have works or it is dead? Someone might think this way, "Well, we can't find approval for our good works before we accept Christ, but once we are saved, we get to work."

There is truth in this sentiment; however, there is also a trap. It is true that our faith will produce works, but which works are the best works to be working in? We can fall into the trap of being about works *for* the Lord. These works can undermine our faith in His grace because we are working *for* His blessing, and working *for* His approval again. God's grace has provided the works, but it's not our works. Let me explain.

We have been made complete in Christ (Col. 2:10). We've been given the very life of Christ (Col. 3:4). The life we now live, we live by faith in His grace. We no longer walk predominantly according to the course, wisdom, and understanding of this world; we live by faith. What is this faith walk? *It is a grace walk that stays grace minded.*

## Grace Minded

When James says that faith without works is dead, this means that faith alone has no power in this life to accomplish the will of God. In other words, it remains dormant, unmoved, unused, and untapped. We can live our entire Christian lives missing His grace by being dominated by the flesh and naturalism. We are called to a new kingdom. In this kingdom, there are new rules of engagement. *It is a kingdom based completely in the finished work of Christ.*

The question then becomes how do we access, activate, and empower this walk? According to scripture, our faith is made alive by acknowledging it. Listen to this verse:

> "...that the sharing of *your faith may become effective by the acknowledgment of every good thing which is in you in Christ Jesus.*" (Philemon 1:6, emphasis added)

Our faith becomes effective, powerful, alive, and activated when we acknowledge, assert, and stand in the truth brought to us in Jesus (John 1:17). Our works are not the good things we try to do *for* God; they are the good things that *come from* us because we are standing in His grace. It is because we are staying *grace minded* that our thoughts, beliefs, and actions take on spiritual life and manifestation. When we believe the right things about what has happened to us, and belong to us because of being born of God, we'll live in the right things. When we see Jesus in us, we'll be transformed in our living, as this verse proclaims:

> "But we all, with unveiled face, beholding as in a mirror the glory of the Lord, *are being transformed into the same image from glory to glory, just as by the Spirit of the Lord.*" (2 Cor. 3:18, emphasis added)

The true work of every believer is to live in His grace and fight the right fight, which is to stay *grace minded!*

## The Wrong Fight

We often fight the wrong fight. We try to clean up the old man; we concentrate our efforts on keeping the law, thinking that is what pleases the Lord. When we focus our attention on our works under the law, it makes us *sin conscious.*

There is no power to overcome sin by looking at it. This may explain why we live weak, defeated, and usually guilt ridden Christian lives. Our fight is not trying to overcome our flesh directly. Our fight is to stay focused on Jesus, to let His life and peace rule our hearts. When we do this, we automatically override sin nature by being full of the divine nature:

> "I say then: *walk in the Spirit, and you shall not fulfill the lust of the flesh.*" (Ga 5:16, emphasis added)

These verses speak to the fight that Paul wrote about (emphasis added):

> *"Fight the good fight of faith, lay hold on eternal life,* to which you were also called and have confessed the good confession in the presence of many witnesses." (1Ti 6:12)

> *"I have fought the good fight,* I have finished the race, *I have kept the faith."* (2Ti 4:7)

The fight is to lay hold of the eternal truth and grace brought to us in Christ Jesus. We are to confess, agree with, acknowledge, assert, and stand in the new creation—His finished work! We are to keep our faith in His grace always. We are saved by seeing Jesus in us, and being *Christ conscious.*

This fight is the work of faith involved with a two-sided coin. On one side is faith, and on the other side is the fight (or works) to stay *grace minded.* The work we have is to overcome our sin nature, and natural default, that thinks naturally every day. We must remind ourselves of these things daily: we are forgiven, we are given the gift of righteousness, and we have the Holy Spirit dwelling in us to do the very things Jesus said we'd do. We fight to see ourselves the way God sees us in Christ, despite our failings, shortcomings, and sin issues.

It takes faith to understand that His grace has already given to us all things that pertain to life and godliness (2 Pet. 1:3). It takes faith to understand that the sins I've just committed are already covered, and I thank Him they are forgiven (Heb. 10:14). It takes faith to realize that everything that is according to God's will, and promised in scripture, is "yes and amen" to me (2 Cor. 1:19).

This is a battle, this is a fight, and it takes work on our part to acknowledge, assert and stand in the things of Christ, because He's in us. God will not overpower our will; all of the grace of God is subject to our desire to concentrate in these truths:

> "Now to Him who is able to do exceedingly abundantly above all that we ask or think, *according to the power that works in us...*" (Eph 3:20, emphasis added)

## In Conclusion

We are not saved by any works of our own; we stand in salvation, completely in the finished work of Christ. When we become born again, we must fight (or work) to stay grace minded. It is walking in the Spirit, by His grace, which produces the fruit (or works) that please God. We must acknowledge, assert, and stand in the things given to us in Christ Jesus. Otherwise, they lay dormant within us because the things of God are subject to us. It is what we believe that determines how we live. If we believe the right things, we'll produce the right works.

We don't work for our salvation. We don't work for God's blessing. We don't work for God's approval. We were given the gift of righteousness when we accepted Jesus as our Lord. We now stand blessed, saved, and approved always in Him, and it's not based on how good we are. It is all based on how good Jesus is.

We must choose to stay grace minded, and that takes work on our part. This work activates the truth that sets us free in Him. Therefore, faith without works is dead, as in powerless to change our lives, or for us to become an effective witness in this life.

We can only come to understand these things as we embrace the truth on both sides of the salvation issue: are we saved by works and conditions, or are we saved by faith alone? We are not saved by works, but once we are saved, we work the works of Christ in His grace. Amen.

# Chapter XIV

# BLESSED ASSURANCE, OR ETERNAL SECURITY? ONCE SAVED ALWAYS SAVED, OR CAN PEOPLE LOSE THEIR SALVATION?

This is another subject that has created tension in the body of Christ. On the one side, proponents insist that a Christian *can* lose their salvation by deciding to walk away—by willfully turning away from God. Some declare others lost in backsliding because they are committing willful or habitual sin. On the other side, many adamantly claim that once someone is born again and saved, they will always be so.

The scriptures produce this tension, and when we remove it, we find ourselves either to the left or right, resulting in intense conflicts with other Christians.

The scriptures present both of these positions (in my opinion). Here are some of the verses that speak to eternal security, with emphasis added:

> "...having been born again, not of corruptible seed but *incorruptible,* through the word of God which lives and abides forever..." (1Pe 1:23)

> "For by one offering *He has perfected forever* those who are being sanctified." (Heb 10:14)

"This is the bread which came down from heaven--not as your fathers ate the manna, and are dead. *He who eats this bread will live forever.*" (Joh 6:58)

"And a slave does not abide in the house forever, *but a son abides forever.*" (Joh 8:35)

Here are some verses that present losing one's salvation by being cut off, cast out, and being impossible to renew back into repentance (emphasis added):

"Therefore consider the goodness and severity of God: on those who fell, severity; but toward you, goodness, *if you continue in His goodness. Otherwise you also will be cut off.*" (Ro 11:22)

"If anyone does not abide in Me, *he is cast out as a branch and is withered; and they gather them and throw them into the fire, and they are burned.*" (Joh 15:6)

"*For it is impossible for those who were once enlightened,* and have tasted of the heavenly gift, and *were made partakers of the Holy Ghost,* And have tasted the good word of God, and the powers of the world to come, *If they shall fall away, to renew them again unto repentance;* seeing they crucify to themselves the Son of God afresh, and put him to an open shame." (Heb. 6: 4-6)

I have heard interpretations over the years from one side and then the other. It seems that we often "dance" to make those passages that appear to contradict our position line up. Sometimes it is like forcing a square peg in a round hole. Elaborate explanations are given to bring harmony to one side or the other.

In considering this particular issue, it seems quite impossible to us that both sides of salvation could be true. How can one be eternally secure and also lose their salvation? This tension in scripture seems to be *irreconcilable*; yet, if we remain faithful to both, wouldn't we have to assert that they are?

How can it be true that once we are saved, we are always saved; but we can lose our salvation? How can it be true that once grafted in, we can be cut off again; yet, we are perfected forever? How can we be born of incorruptible seed (which means we cannot be corrupted); then, because we don't abide in Him be cast away?

Many simply decide that one side is correct and the other is misinterpreted, misapplied, taken out of context, and poorly presented. We of course, believe this about the ones who stand on the opposite side of what we affirm.

## Conditions?

Most of the argument centers upon whether our salvation has *conditions*. Do we see in scripture that salvation is unconditional?

Here are some verses that express conditions, with emphasis added:

> "But whoever denies Me before men, him *I will also deny before My Father who is in heaven"* (Matt. 10: 33.

> "But Jesus said to him, *'No one, having put his hand to the plow, and looking back,* is fit for the kingdom of God.'" (Lu 9:62)

> "And he who does *not take his cross and follow after Me* is not worthy of Me." (Mt 10:38)

> "So likewise, *whoever of you does not forsake all that he has cannot* be My disciple." (Lu 14:33)

These types of verses imply strongly that we must meet some conditions to be saved (continually): We must profess Christ before men; we must engage in and remain working for the kingdom;

we must take up our cross and follow; and finally (in this set of verses), we must forsake all that we have.

Here are some scriptures that seem to say something quite different (emphasis added):

> "Therefore He is also *able to save to the uttermost* those who come to God through Him, since *He always lives to make intercession for them*." (Heb. 7:25)

> "I am the vine, you are the branches. He who abides in Me, and I in him, bears much fruit; for *without Me you can do nothing*." (Joh 15:5)

> "For by grace you have been saved through faith, *and that not of yourselves; it is the gift of God, not of works, lest anyone should boast.*
> *For we are His workmanship*, created in Christ Jesus for good works, which God prepared beforehand that we should walk in them." (Eph. 2: 8-10)

These verses seem to take the *conditions completely out of our hands,* by saying we are saved to the *uttermost* part of our being. In other words, we have nothing to contribute towards our salvation; furthermore, Jesus said that we can do nothing without Him. Our salvation is stated as a gift, even our faith, lest anyone should boast that he or she had something to do with it.

## Salvation Identities

If we look at some of the identities scripture gives that relate to what salvation is like, maybe that can help inform the debate. First, *marriage* is used to describe our salvation:

> "Therefore, my brethren, you also have become dead to the law through the body of Christ, *that you may*

145

*be married to another—to Him* who was raised from the dead, that we should bear fruit to God." (Ro 7:4, emphasis added)

We all know that marriage is supposed to be for life. Divorce is something only available due to the hardness of men's hearts (Mark 10:4, 5). This would certainly line up with the idea that once we are married to Christ in salvation, it is forever; however, marriages are abandoned, separated from, and divorced. From God's perspective, it's forever; *it is man that brought in brokenness.*

We are called *ambassadors* for Christ. This appointment is for everyone who comes to the Lord. It functions in this way: our *true citizenship* is in heaven while we remain on the earth (Phip. 3:20). We represent Christ to the world. As far as God is concerned, our citizenship in heaven is forever; however, ambassadors do abandon their posts. Some are removed from their appointments; therefore, *from a human perspective, this position can be lost too.*

We are called *sons and daughters.* Once we are born into this world, our father and mother are forever fixed. We may have substitute parents, but our birth parents are never replaced. The scripture refers to us as adopted into the beloved (Eph. 1:5). Once adopted, can someone be removed?

I know that sometimes parents denounce and declare that they have no son or daughter. Jewish conversions to Christ often result in devout Jewish parents doing this. Muslim converts also face this from their devout Muslim parents. *Then, even this identity, from the human side of things, can be lost.*

It seems that as far as human experience, even our most sacred, honored, and supposedly fixed relationships can be broken. Human beings are not trust worthy; there is nothing we can establish that would last forever.

Does God ever break off sacred, honored, and supposedly fixed relationships? We find it so in the Old Testament situation:

"My people are destroyed for lack of knowledge. Because you have rejected knowledge, *I also will reject you* from being priest for Me; *because you have forgotten the law of your God, I also will forget your children.*" (Ho 4:6, emphasis added)

"...therefore behold, *I, even I, will utterly forget you and forsake you,* and the city that I gave you and your fathers, and will cast you out of My presence." (Jer 23:39, emphasis added)

God will not tolerate rebellion, insubordination, disobedience, and rejection forever. There appears to come a time when God rejects, cuts off, and casts away, too. This all changes because of Christ Jesus! God no longer deals with us according to our efforts, but through grace, deals with us according to Jesus' effort.

God at one time dealt with us according to our own works. At one time, we were under the law. God found fault *not* with the law, but with us as Heb. 8:8-13 explains (emphasis added):

*"Because finding fault with them,* He says: "Behold, the days are coming, says the LORD, when *I will make a new covenant* with the house of Israel and with the house of Judah—not according to the covenant that I made with their fathers in the day when I took them by the hand to lead them out of the land of Egypt; *because they did not continue in My covenant, and I disregarded them,* says the LORD.

For this is the covenant that I will make with the house of Israel after those days, says the LORD: *I will put My laws in their mind and write them on their hearts; and I will be their God, and they shall be My people.*

None of them shall teach his neighbor, and none his brother, saying, 'Know the LORD,' *for all shall know Me,* from the least of them to the greatest of them.

For I will be *merciful to their unrighteousness, and their sins and their lawless deeds I will remember no more.*"

In that He says, "A new covenant," *He has made the first obsolete.* Now what is becoming obsolete and growing old is ready to vanish away."

God found fault with us and decided to *remove all the human conditions* for salvation, because we are unable to keep them. The law was given to reveal and expose our sins, so that we would turn to the savior (Gal. 3:24). In the new covenant, the conditions passed from our efforts to Jesus. All of the conditions for salvation, Jesus has met and provided, then turns to us and says, "Come…"

"Come to Me, all you who labor and are heavy laden, *and I will give you rest.***" (**Mt 11:28, emphasis added)

The conditions of salvation have been met in Christ. When we come to Him, we are saved to the *uttermost.* The only condition that remains: "believing in Him!"

"Then they said to Him, "What shall we do, that we may work the works of God?"
Jesus answered and said to them, *"This is the work of God that you believe in Him whom He sent."* (John 6: 28, 29, emphasis added)

Our salvation no longer depends upon conditions set under the law, but completely in His grace. God is giving us everything we could have never achieved under the conditions of the law. Therefore, we can now put away our works, efforts, and burden of trying to keep the law, and look unto Jesus the author and finisher of our faith (Heb. 12:2).

## It's All Based On Believing in Him—Nothing Else

I share this to ask the question; under what condition now would our salvation be lost? Would it be lost by our continual sins?

Would it be lost because we have not confessed all of our sins (I John 1:9)? Since Jesus has paid the price for all of our sins forever, sin is no longer an issue. *What remains is our believing in Him.* If we believe, we shall be saved.

Can someone who is saved, lose their salvation? If it is based upon sinning, the answer is no. Can someone who is saved, lose their salvation based *on turning away from Christ?* If turning away from Christ (as in living for Him in life) would be considered sin, then that too would be covered as sins paid for in the cross; however, it is the rejection of Christ within our heart that cannot be forgiven! If we are not under Christ and covered by His blood, there is no remission of sins. There is only one sin that cannot be forgiven—rejecting Jesus! Can someone who is born again commit this sin?

In light of that question, when we become born again, we become *a new creation.* In the new creation, all things have become new:

> "Therefore, if anyone is in Christ, *he is a new creation*; old things have passed away; behold, *all things have become new.*" (2Co 5:17, emphasis added)

In our new creation status, we are born of God and have received *the divine nature (His seed) within that cannot sin.* Listen to this verse:

> "*Whoever has been born of God does not sin, for His seed remains in him; and he cannot sin,* because he has been born of God." (1Jo 3:9, emphasis added)

For someone to be born of God, and then later turn away from Him, that would mean their *carnal nature* has become dominate. In turning away, are we addressing a life not lived in the Spirit in this world? Or, are we addressing a heart's desire to absolutely reject Christ, after having accepted Him?

Remember, the spirit within them cannot sin and would not turn away—ever.

> "For the flesh lusts against the Spirit, and the Spirit against the flesh; and these are contrary to one another, so that you do not do the things that you wish." (Ga 5:17, emphasis added)

## One Conclusion:

Is it possible for someone who is born of God, to live carnally and be dominated by it? Absolutely, it is possible, and quite a travesty, knowing that our Lord paid the price for our salvation, liberty, and victory in the Spirit (Phil. 4:13). The truth is, however, that many brothers and sisters in Christ have lived defeated lives. Many live in guilt and shame. Many remain under condemnation, because even as Christians, sins still manifest and often dominate.

Some have been so defeated by their failure to overcome, they have left the faith (shipwrecked), believing they are unworthy, displeasing to God, and that God has rejected them. The scriptures reveal that condemnation kills, but the Spirit gives life (2 Cor. 3:6). The simple truth is: not all believers live to and experience genuine life in the Spirit.

> "There is therefore now no condemnation to those who are in Christ Jesus, who do not walk according to the flesh, but according to the Spirit." (Ro 8:1, emphasis added)

When we became born again, we were conveyed into a new kingdom based solely in God's grace (Col. 1:13). Our sin—past, present, and future—were paid for through Christ's atonement once and for all time:

"But this Man, after *He had offered one sacrifice for sins forever*, sat down at the right hand of God." (Heb 10:12, emphasis added)

*"For by one offering He has perfected forever* those who are being sanctified." (Heb 10:14, emphasis added)

This means that our Lord provided forgiveness, not just for sins, *but for sin nature itself!* When we come to Him, our *old man passes away*, and we are to consider it dead:

*"For you died*, and your life is hidden with Christ in God." (Col 3:3, emphasis added)

It appears that the testimony and teaching found in the New Testament, regarding *the possibility* of losing one's salvation, is very small (in volume). If we died to the old man according to scripture, even though we may live to it for the rest of our lives, our life is still hidden in Christ our Lord. We may be saved with nothing to show for it (no rewards), but we are saved, nevertheless. I believe this is the meaning of the following passage from I Cor. 3:12-15 (emphasis added):

"Now if anyone builds on this foundation with gold, silver, precious stones, *wood, hay, straw*, each one's work will become clear; for the Day will declare it, because it will be revealed by fire; and the fire will test each one's work, *of what sort it is*.

If anyone's work which he has built on endures, he will receive a reward.

If anyone's work is burned, *he will suffer loss; but he himself will be saved*, yet so as through fire.

**The Tension Still Remains:**

There are still those few passages that warn us as Christians, such as this one:

> "So then, because you are lukewarm, and neither cold nor hot, *I will vomit you out of My mouth.*" (Re 3:16, emphasis added)

In another place, the Word of God says that He *will not blot out our names* from the book of life, if the condition is met. This means it is possible to have our names blotted out from the Book of Life!

> "He who overcomes shall be clothed in white garments, *and I will not blot out his name from the Book of Life;* but I will confess his name before My Father and before His angels." (Re 3:5, emphasis added)

The point this makes is obvious from the following verse:

> "*And anyone not found written in the Book of Life was cast into the lake of fire.*" (Re 20:15, emphasis added)

The tension in this issue still remains, as we must affirm the Word of God on both sides. Somehow, someway, eternal security is offered forever, while the possibility of one being cast out, cut off, and their name blotted from the Book of Life exists too.

God is not schizophrenic, nor does He contradict Himself. The depth this tension brings may lead us to things beyond our spiritual understanding at present; however, there are some answers that may exist to alleviate some of the tension, without denying scripture to do it. For example:

What if everyone's name is written in the Book of Life, since Jesus died for all? When someone rejects Christ and dies that is when their name is blotted from it. Then, when judgment is exercised, their name would not be found. This seems plausible but this verse seems to indicate otherwise:

"All who dwell on the earth will worship him, *whose names have not been written in the Book of Life of the Lamb* slain from the foundation of the world." (Re 13:8, emphasis added)

Another example: What if God's vomiting the lukewarm condition out of His mouth doesn't mean eternal condemnation? What if it just means the rejection of their life's behavior?

Some kind of answer or "dance" may actually be found for every verse in apparent contradiction to eternal security's position; yet, it may not be a completely satisfying answer. What if, in the realm of God's Spirit, there is a way for both sides of this issue to be true?

What if, God in His relationship to each person, knowing their heart and in His love, justice, and mercy, still finds their rejection unacceptable? The warnings are clear and really unmistakable.

We certainly all agree that God provides extremely solid assurance (security), even to the point of *sealing* one in the Spirit for their salvation—guaranteeing it!

"In Him you also trusted, after you heard the word of truth, the gospel of your salvation; in whom also, having believed, *you were sealed with the Holy Spirit of promise, who is the guarantee of our inheritance* until the redemption of the purchased possession, to the praise of His glory." (Eph. 1:13, 14, emphasis added)

## Conclusion:

As long as we remain in the tension that the scriptures provide concerning our salvation, we will remain closer to the truth and each other. It is when we discard one side over the other that we become in tension with each other. It is possible to embrace "once saved; always saved," and still acknowledge that the scriptures do warn us severely that salvation can be lost? How can they both be true?

I don't personally know. I see a little here and there, but by staying in the tension I am far less dogmatic, threatened, or argumentative with people I disagree with on this subject. Since I see both sides, the only ones I tend to disagree with are the ardent proponents with the dogmatic flavor that have completely removed the tension.

My journey started in the camp I was brought up in, believing we can lose our salvation. In fact, some in that camp believe it can be lost simply by backsliding even a little. At this point, I've swung almost to the other end, and have declared in sermons that we are forgiven forever! Nevertheless, I am still uncomfortable with stating, as many others do, that we are "once saved; always saved."

God's depth is unfathomable; yet, it is His gift to us to know Him and be filled with His Spirit. It is His will that we be filled with His wisdom and understanding:

> "For this reason we also, since the day we heard it, do not cease to pray for you, and to ask that *you may be filled with the knowledge of His will in all wisdom and spiritual understanding...*" (Col 1:9, emphasis added)

What this means to me, in regards to the tension in this particular issue, is to not remove it, and find myself to the left or the right of it. This would further mean that my meditations remain faithful to sustain the passages that reveal God's great security for every believer, while at the same time, remain open to the fact that other revelations show that salvation can be lost.

It is a crazy place to be, and it challenges my understanding, reasoning, and sense of clarity; yet, I still believe with the fruit, the examples in this book, that it is the better place to be. The Spirit reveals, makes known, and brings understanding that is beyond our human ability to grasp. The answer to this issue may be astounding at some point, how both sides of this could be true.

For now, I certainly understand that as far as God is concerned, there is *no possible way* for us to lose our salvation. It is incorruptible, it is divine, it is forever established, and it is God who provided it and sustains it. Jesus is the author and finisher of our faith!

The fact remains, as with other sacred, honored, and supposedly fixed relationships, that human beings manage to somehow break them. *Is it possible that as far as God's involvement, our salvation cannot be broken, but as far as human will, God will not override it—no matter what?*

The whole purpose of life, creation, the universe, and man being given dominion, is our free will to choose. Does this mean that once we choose God and His salvation, we no longer have the potential to leave? Does this mean that in this life, once we are born again, we lose our freedom to step away?

I have to admit that when it comes to eternity, the idea that we could step away, leave God, or fall away, is abhorrent. When I envision eternity, knowing how easy it is to sin as a Christian in this life, the idea that my relationship to God could fail just scares me to the core. I don't want to believe it's possible, once we leave this natural fallen condition, that we could ever fall again. I don't believe it, and I don't believe the scriptures even hint at that future scenario.

There is, however, this time in life; this is the battleground that determines the eternal destination of everyone. Once this battle is over, I believe it is over forever! While this battle continues, even with the massive, clear, and understandable security we've been promised in scripture, there still remains the other side. The verses that cut off, cast away, blot out, or spew from God's mouth, still state vivid, understandable, and frightening warnings. How can they both be true? I don't know, but I will remain in the tension, although far to the one side, closer to the "once saved; always saved" position.

# CONCLUDING REMARKS

I have endeavored to flesh out the point of this book. I have addressed some major issues of teaching in the body of Christ. Some may not appreciate where I come out when understanding these areas (while remaining in the tension), but they may still grow in understanding their own outcome. *Tension in the scriptures must be recognized as intended for the purposes I've put forth and more.* If we have the mistaken idea that God's word is seamless, serene, and altogether smooth, we are going to find ourselves missing a lot.

I'm not saying for a moment that God's word isn't perfect, eternally connected in purity and peace, or inerrant. I believe it is God breathed, fully inspired from the first verse to the last (in the original languages). What I am saying is that our conceptions, understandings, wisdom to grasp, are tainted by our sin nature.

I don't believe Jesus experienced the tension I'm addressing because He was sinless, did not have a carnal mind, and was *One* with the Father. The conflict is within us, as we try to take in the divine. We are finite beings coming to know, coming to learn, and coming to be enlightened by the infinite One.

The Word of God is Spirit, truth, life, and the way. *It requires the work of the Holy Spirit to reveal it to our spirit.* The carnal mind is enmity against the Spirit and the mind of Christ (Rom. 8:7). The natural man is bound by naturalism and cannot comprehend the supernatural life of divinity. When one-dimensional thinking and believing is exposed to multidimensional revelations, it is going to create tension inside of us.

Instead of thinking the tension is wrong, we need *to embrace it and acknowledge its work in us, to bring us to the place where true revelation answers can manifest.* When we do this, as I have explained, it keeps us on the straight and narrow life of the Spirit. It is important to accept this phenomenon as authentic, expecting it, and then resting in it; it will help us be more receptive. It will help us not to make the mistake of trying to relieve the scriptural tensions *on our own.* When we remove them, we end up faltering in error, misunderstanding, and off to the left or right of the issues.

When the Spirit brings revelation to answer why the tension exists, and how both biblical statements are true, the tension is removed by becoming aware and enlightened to Spiritual things.

There is a reason why Paul wrote:

> "Now we have received, *not the spirit of the world,* but the Spirit who is from God, *that we might know the things that have been freely given to us by God.*
> These things we also speak, *not in words which man's wisdom teaches* but which the Holy Spirit teaches, *comparing spiritual things with spiritual.*
> *But the natural man does not receive the things of the Spirit of God, for they are foolishness to him; nor can he know them, because they are spiritually discerned.*
> But he who is spiritual judges all things, yet he himself is rightly judged by no one. For 'who has known the mind of the LORD that he may instruct Him?' *But we have the mind of Christ."* (I Cor. 2: 12-16, emphasis added)

When we consider the things of the Spirit, we struggle, stress to comprehend, and experience this tension, because of our need to renew our mind according to God's Word (Rom. 12:2). This renewal process is not *just* memorizing, or having a good knowledge of what the scriptures teach. It is seeing things the way Christ does with spiritual eyes and ears.

Spiritual depth is not measured by how much we think we know, how many right answers we think we can produce, or by how much scripture we can quote. Spiritual depth is the *growing awareness of the gift of righteousness in His grace* (Eph. 5:14); it is putting on the mind of Christ and walking in the Spirit (Gal. 3:27). These things are not works that we can accomplish or take credit for (Eph. 2:9). This is the work of the Spirit. It all centers on who Christ is to us in our focused relationship to Him.

> "But we all, with unveiled face, beholding as in a mirror the glory of the Lord, *are being transformed into the same image from glory to glory, just as by the Spirit of the Lord.*" (2 Cor. 3:18, emphasis added)

Just to be clear, the tension is *not actually* in the scripture, it is in us trying to understand the scripture. It is what we experience as we embrace the truth found in it. It is what happens within us as the divine life becomes brighter and brighter until the full day (Proverbs 4:18). It is accurate to say, "The tension is in the scriptures," from our perspective; therefore, we can also say, "It is not whether we should experience tension, but which is the best tension to remain in."

There is, in truth, right and wrong tension for us as Christians. It is the effort of this book to help us discern the difference, and see the benefits of remaining in the right tension, while at the same time, helping us to get out of the wrong ones. Let the peace of Christ rule our hearts, and keep us in His divine tension.

This final passage may be familiar to many, but I think it provides confirmation and a witness that our spiritual journey, our understanding of God, and our study of scripture, are all filled, and intended to be so, with godly tension. Listen to 2 Cor. 6:3-10 and, of course, with emphasis added:

> We give no offense in anything, that our ministry may not be blamed.

But in all things we commend ourselves as ministers of God: in much patience, in tribulations, in needs, in distresses, in stripes, in imprisonments, in tumults, in labors, in sleeplessness, in fasting; by purity, by knowledge, by longsuffering, by kindness, by the Holy Spirit, by sincere love, by the word of truth, by the power of God, by the armor of righteousness on the right hand and on the left, *by honor and dishonor, by evil report and good report; as deceivers, and yet true; as unknown, and yet well known; as dying, and behold we live; as chastened, and yet not killed; as sorrowful, yet always rejoicing; as poor, yet making many rich; as having nothing, and yet possessing all things.*

## Contact Pastor and Author?

I'd be honored and privileged if the reader would like to contact me about anything concerning the content of this book. You may do so at my website: *Lordsbdt.com* or email: Leroyfluff32@ hotmail.com

# BIBLIOGRAPHY

Note: Every one of these books engages, employs, reveals, and applies the tension found in scripture.

Rich Christians In The Age Of Hunger by Ron Sider, Publisher: Thomas Nelson; Copyright 1978, Printed in USA.

Living In The Balance of Grace And Faith, by Andrew Wommack, Publisher: Harrison House Inc (June 4, 2011), printed in USA.

The Christian's Secret To A Happy Life, by Hannah Whitall Smith, Publisher: Revell (December 1, 2012), printed in USA.

The Case For Christ, by Lee Strobel, Publisher: Zondervan (December 24, 2013), printed in USA.

New Creation Realities, by E.W. Kenyon, Publisher: Kenyon's Gospel Publishing Society, Inc. Copyright 2000, printed in USA.

Everybody Is Normal Till You Get To Know Them, John Orberg, Publisher: Zondervan 1994, printed in USA.

A Skeptic's Search for God: Convincing Evidence for His Existence, by Ralph O. Muncaster, Publisher: Harvest House Publishers; First Edition edition (May 1, 2002), printed USA.

Boundaries: When to Say Yes, When to Say No-To Take Control of Your Life, by Henry Cloud & John Townsend, Publisher: Zondervan 1994, printed in USA.

Dare to Discipline, by James Dobson, Publisher: Tyndale House, Publishers; Reprint edition (1975), printed in USA.

Celebration of Discipline: The Path to Spiritual Growth, by Richard J. Foster, Publisher: Harper, San Francisco; 1st edition (1988), printed in USA.

# ABOUT THE AUTHOR

Pastor B. D. Tate has served in the
Christian church for over forty
years—from youth group leader
and Sunday school teacher to men's
group leadership to assistant pastor
and, finally, as a senior pastor for
twenty-eight years. He has been
married for thirty-seven years to
Valerie, with four grown children

and ten grandchildren. He has been involved with Assemblies of
God, Christian Missionary and Alliance, Word of Faith, United
Methodist, and nondenominational churches. He received his
MDiv degree from Eastern Baptist Theological Seminary (1992).
He was ordained in the UMC (1996) and continues to serve as
founding pastor of Lord of Lords Bible Community Church, where
he has taught for the past eleven years. He has written over one
hundred booklets, many Bible studies, and is published on his
website, Lordsbdt.com . He is a graduate of Penn State University,
where he played quarterback for the late Coach Joe Paterno.